Jill
Thankyou for all
your help with
everything !
Go forth & prosper x
Lots of love,
Kerry xx

The Gift

Kirsty McKinnon

First published in 2007
© Copyright 2007
Kirsty McKinnon

The right of Kirsty McKinnon to be identified as the author of this work has been asserted by her in accordance with Copyright, Designs and Patents Act 1998. All rights reserved. No reproduction, copy or transmission of this publication may be made without written permission. No paragraph of this publication may be reproduced, copied or transmitted save with the written permission or in accordance with the provisions of the Copyright Act 1956 (as amended).

Any person who does any unauthorised act in relation to this publication may be liable to criminal prosecution and civil claims for damage. Although every effort has been made to assure the accuracy of the information contained in this guide as of the date of publication, nothing herein should be construed as giving specific treatment advice. In addition, the application of the techniques to specific circumstances can present complex issues that are beyond the scope of this guide. This publication is intended to provide general information pertaining to developing these skills.

ISBN-13 9781904312284 ISBN 1904312284

MX Publishing Ltd, 10 Kingfisher Close, Stanstead Abbotts, Hertfordshire, SG12 8LQ – www.mxpublishing.co.uk

Acknowledgements

To **every single** student and client. Thanks, you have taught me a MAHOUSIVE amount.
For my teachers, Tad and Adriana James. For everyone in nlpcoaching, thanks. (Conor – thanks for the smoothies!)

To Ailie who has been fantastic in our business and has shaped it into a bigger business. As a chief sorter outerer/editor/proof-reader you have certainly sorted stuff out (although – where's the time travel machine?)

To Mum and Dad who know that I will never grow up. For Russell who agrees.

And most of all thank you to Iain (who assumes crash position whenever I come up with another idea!) who I love more than sparkly shoes, Battenburg cake AND pink.
Thanks for being the best support anyone could ever have. I love you.
This is for you.

"Everybody smiles in the same language"

Mother Teresa

Contents

Introduction 10
Overview of NLP 12

Part 1 – The Stories 23
Positive learning's *Pam Wiggins* 24
Chuckle knuckles *Kevin Charlton* 26
Why oh why? *Damian Culhane* 27
Move over Tiger *Michael Gallagher* 30
Storming the flat *Emma Jones* 31
An elephant, a skinny latte and...*Julie Evers* 33
Made from Girders *Hilary Thain* 36
To hoe or not to hoe *Gary Anderson* 37
Is it OK to be OK? *Mawgen Schoeman* 39
Fizzy sweets, cats and..... *Osmaan Sharif* 41
Fight or flight *Karen McGowan* 44
Successful Successes *Ron Symington* 47
Educating Education *Clair Donegan & Julia Armstrong* 49
What procrastination? *Christine Mclean* 51
Hello up there? *Penny Bedford* 53
Because we can we know *Janet Courtenay* 55
Mum's the word *Anonymous* 56

I mean business *Christine Mclean*	57
Radio calling *Jude Eller*	59
I want to sort my sh*t out *Tracey Underwood*	61
Bed, breakfast & life coaching *Carol Monteith*	64
It's a small world *Erica Course*	66
All aboard *Carol Harte*	68
Upgrading life *Rahul Patil*	69
The visioning anchor continuum *David Kelly*	71
Wobblegob and weightloss *Colette Boyden*	74
The jobs yours *Anon*	76
Using your loaf *Michael Gallagher*	77
Shine a light *Jude Eller*	79
Outcome of goal setting *Mark Thompson*	82
Reporting Dyslexia *Olive Hickmott*	84
How not to get sick *Lorna Green*	86
The futures bright *Karen Mason*	88
Stuck in a moment *Mark Robinson*	90
The illusion of reality *Nisha Kissoon*	94
I'll do it my way *Hilary Thain*	99
That was easy! *Ailie Duncan*	105
Fore! *Bill Cole*	108
Metaphorically speaking *Ann Douglas*	110
Lights, camera action *Kevin Charlton*	113
Presenting Magically *Steve Broom*	115
TLTing at windmills *David Kelly*	118
Spider schmider *Simon Almond*	119
Still no collywobbles *Frances Devlin*	120

I'm in the money! *Susan Perry*	122
Any dream will do *Rahul Patil*	123

Part 2

How to do what they did	125
It's an inside job – the mindset and key frames	127
The "L" word – language and its power	133
Outcomes	151
I'm like this person, I like this person - Rapport	158
Hear no evil, see no evil - Representational systems	164
The eyes have it	172
Planes, trains, chocolate and spiders - Submodalities and their techniques	182
Magic Buttons - Anchors & how to be in charge of your state	194
Come Fly with me -Time Line therapy™	206
The Value in knowing your values	216
Applications	224

Introduction

When the idea for this book came along I think it was a long time coming. A few people had asked if we catalogue all the successes and results from students and, yes, they were stored in my inbox, however they weren't pulled together and shared.

So here it is.

We get emails, letters and phone calls of amazing results every day. What people have achieved choices they have taken and changes they have made.

This is amazing stuff.

Some people wait on their crisis in order to start living their lives; they are happy surviving rather than thriving. We get one chance; our view is to live it fantastically. I personally want to get to my last breath and think – wow!

I wanted to bring NLP to life. Every course we see students work on all the techniques together and love the results. It's not until you start putting it all into action that it starts to make sense.

It seems that people can be hesitant or sometimes fearful of the likes of NLP, anything to do with "the brain" has a stigma attached to it. It's no surprise really, we are born with this fantastic tool and no one actually tells us how to use it. Scientists say we use only 5%. Well that's a long disputed fact; it's safe to say that the potential of the human brain is infinite.

No-one is given an instruction manual for their mind at birth, and so we go through life programming it in a certain way. We have 60,000 thoughts a day, how many of *those* are conscious? Therefore if we are already programming it unconsciously then surely we can programme our unconscious mind consciously? NLP allows us to programme our mind in a way that benefits us.

For me, NLP allows us to take a good look at ourselves, to understand what is happening internally – it's like taking out your brain and observing it for the first time and promoting a huge self awareness.

How this book works.

The first part of the book documents how people have put some of the techniques into action. Some of the stories talk about techniques; others talk about a certain mindset that for them is key.

The second part gives you an idea of the different NLP techniques and how to use them. There are simple exercises for you to complete (these are denoted by **"STTTTRREETCH")** to ensure you reap the benefits yourself!

Enjoy

What is NLP?

Can it be any broader a title? Indeed, what is it? I don't actually think it makes it any easier to "deabbreviate" it – its Neuro Linguistic Programming.

I remember when I first started to talk about what I did and a lot of people thought I was doing work on computers. Well, we like to call it our neck top computer! As I said earlier, our brain is a phenomenal tool however no one tells us how to use it and that essentially is what NLP is all about. It's an instruction manual for the mind; it allows us to programme our minds in a way that is beneficial to us. It believes in the premise that if you are not getting the results you want, you can change your thinking and ultimately your behaviour.

What's in the name?

Neuro
Neuro applies to the way in which we experience the world. We experience it through our 5 senses:
Visual – seeing, Auditory – hearing, Kinaesthetic – feeling, Olfactory – smelling, Gustatory – tasting. The senses are the means by which we interact and experience our world. We then take these experiences and filter it in our minds and translate it to conscious and unconscious thought.
Linguistic
This is the language that we use. We communicate consciously and unconsciously and only 7 % of our communication is our language; 93% is unconscious – our physiology and tone of

voice. The language we use is paramount to the success we can achieve. Our language creates the world that we live in. Most of us think our language actually describes our life, in actual fact it is the start of the creation of our life and what we attract. We are all magnets attracting our thoughts – our thoughts become physical realities.

The majority of what comes out of our mouths is unconscious – we open our mouths and speak and then, perhaps, think of the consequences. We need to be able to use our language consciously to enable us to achieve the results that we want. The language we use is exceedingly important.

Programming
This is the "how". How do we do what we do? Just like a computer each of us runs certain programmes to produce our behaviours. Using NLP you can find out what programmes you run and what results they are producing. If these programmes aren't working for us, then we can change them.

Anything you can do I can do better!

The essence of NLP starts with modelling. If someone is doing something well, as can we. We can work out the person's strategies, values, attitudes and when we have all the information we can install this information in self by using the techniques of NLP.

The founders of NLP, Richard Bandler and John Grinder spent their time modelling excellent individuals to work out what they were doing and, more importantly, *how* they were doing it. They wanted to know the difference that made the difference.

People like Virginia Satir (family therapist), Milton Erikson (hypnotherapist), and Fritz Perls (gestalt therapy) were the first to be modelled.

For me, NLP is that instruction manual for the mind. The language element is increasingly important; if you want to change the results in your life then you need to change the language that you use.

Our internal world

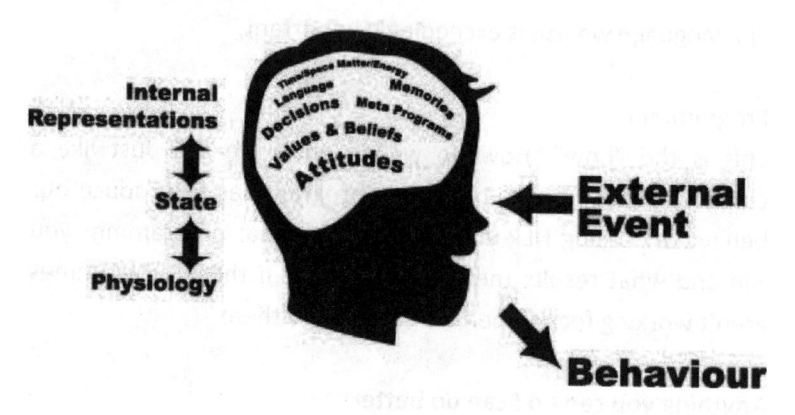

Internal Representations
↕
State
↕
Physiology

Brain contents: Time/Space Matter/Energy, Language, Memories, Decisions, Meta Programs, Values & Beliefs, Attitudes

← **External Event**

↘ **Behaviour**

This is the **NLP Communication model.** We are inundated with information on a daily basis. Every second around 2 million bits of information per second is processed, obviously it would be too much for our minds to cope with if you were consciously aware of this information. Our unconscious minds do this process. Can you imagine!?

According to the Hungarian Biologist, Mihaly Csikszentmihalyi we filter that information to 134 bits per second. Now that's a heck of a filtration system! 0.0067% of what we COULD see we see. We are in a very commercial world; we are immersed with technology – IPODS, Nintendo Wiis, HDTV, and BlackBerry's, phones – which suffuses us with a lot of information.

Scientists say now that biologically, the brain processes 400 billion bits of information per second, but is only aware of 2,000 bits at any one time-usually information about our environment, body, and time.

Just what is the brain perceiving that we are not "seeing" or integrating?

Deleting, Distorting and generalising.

Our filters do the process of deleting, distorting and generalising. Everyone's filters are unique and handle everything that comes in from the outside world. Your filters are your way of making sense of what you are experiencing. They include what you believe, what you want, what you remember and what is important to you. These can change over time so your map of the world changes too.

The information that passes from the external world through your filters is held as an internal representation. These internal representations are our thoughts made up of pictures, feelings, sounds smells and tastes.

This internal representation determines your state and your physiology and, ultimately, your behaviour.

Your state is your internal emotional condition. Your physiology is your *body language* which includes your posture, breathing and facial expressions. Your behaviour is the actions you take in your outside world. All of these are inter related. Your physiology and state can affect your internal representations and your internal representations can affect your physiology and behaviour. By changing our internal world we can change our behaviour, and our life.

STTTRRREEEEttttCH

Think of a maths problem, sit down with your head held low with your tongue hanging out and your shoulders slouched. Go for it, now how are you getting on?

Now, sit up, back straight and shoulders back. Smile on your face with a comfortable erect posture and look at the problem again! Easier huh? Your posture had an effect on the way in which you could think and tackle the problem.

Another one? Well, think of the New Zealand rugby union team and their prematch performance of the traditional Maori dance, the Haka. Think of their physiology and facial expressions, feel the confidence ooze from every pore and assume "Haka stance" (come on now! Haka time!). Get yourself into the state and imagine the opposing team watching your war cry. Be strong, be powerful. Now, think of a time that made you feel slightly anxious, you can't do it can you? Your physiology has affected your state.

Have a look at the below, I think it's a great representation of deletions and distortions!

Our ucoscniouns mnid geos touhrgh the pcorcess of detinleg, distornitg and genalierisng. We hvae to sceern the majority of dtaa that cemos to us. The fsrit way our bairn sotps srosney ovaolerd is through dleteion.
Aoccdrnig to a rscheearch at Cmabrigde Uinervtisy, it deosn't mttaer in what order the ltteers in a word are, the only iprmoatnt tihhg is that the frist and lsat ltteer be in the rghit pclae. The rset can be a taotl mses and you can still raed it wouthit a porbelm. This is bcuseae the human mind deos not raed ervery lteter by istlef, but the word as a wlohe. Amzanig huh?

Deletions

The first way our brain stops sensory overload is through deletion. Although a lot of information comes into our brain we cut out some of it and everything that is deleted falls out of your conscious awareness. Deletion is a process by which we pay attention to certain dimensions of our experience and exclude others. It can be useful, or not depending on the application. Deletion reduces the world to a size in which we are comfortable handling. We delete all the time, (bit of a generalisation!) e.g. remember times when you are in a crowded room and you are focussing in on one person only and deleting the other noise around you. That's when deleting is useful. By deleting information from our language, we can change the aspect and meaning of what we communicate.

Distortions

Distortions are where we make shifts in the sensory data that arrives – where we create or transform the information. You may distort what you see, hear or feel. It is where we alter data so that it fits with our preconceptions.
Research indicates that only 20% of the information we have comes from external cues, and 80% from existing memories, attitudes and filters. Again this is useful, or not depending on the circumstances. The ability to create and transform information is what great artists of our time are able to do; the ability to distort the message on someone's face to mean something entirely different is a downside of distortion.

Generalisations

This is when we group an experience or situation into a similar class or group.
When you are a child a useful way of learning is generalising,
E.g. when we learn not to put our fingers in a plug and then we learn that ALL plugs should be avoided. Imagine you are walking down the road and you see a dog. You have seen one before so you have a word for it. Your brain goes through an unconscious process to say "right, there's an animal with a tail and 4 legs, I have seen one before and I know that it makes a barking sound. I shall put that in the broad category of dogs – large and small"
If that dog then starts to "neigh" is it still a dog???

This process can help a lot; imagine having to learn a new word, or vocabulary, every time we come across something new, I reckon that would become quite exhausting.

Generalisations can be linked with beliefs too, and can be limiting. If you are prone to generalising you might say something like "that last relationship was bad and I was treated badly therefore all relationships are bad ". This belief structure could limit us in a way in which we then don't want to have a relationship.

By noticing how much you generalise (you can recognise this with language patterns – chapter 3) you can begin to notice how much information you are ignoring.

Who runs the ship?

It's important to note that within NLP we work a lot with the unconscious mind. As you can see from the filters and processes of deleting, distorting and generalising a lot of the work that we do is completed at the unconscious level. Our unconscious mind is valuable although some people don't even know they have one!

The analogy that works well is that of a ship. If our conscious mind is the Captain and our unconscious the crew – who runs the ship? Yes, the crew! (All those who said captain – 10 press ups!). The captain gives the orders however it is the crew that actually runs the ship. And what happens when there is "disagreement" between the captain and the ship? Mutiny!!!

That's what can happen within our bodies when the conscious and unconscious mind don't see eye to eye. It's important to be in tune with our unconscious mind, this is the domain of the feelings. The conscious mind is the thinker; the unconscious mind is the feeler. You can tell those people who are not in touch with their conscious mind as they are not in touch with their feelings.

The laws

There are certain beliefs that are very empowering and assist you in looking at the world in an encouraging way. We call them the **presuppositions of NLP**; they are not facts however we presuppose that they are true.

Have respect for different models of the world.

Everybody has a different way of thinking; it's what makes us all unique. You may disagree with others values or belief systems however it is more empowering to respect the fact that everyone is different and has a different model of the world. This allows us to move on and be effective in our communication with people.

The meaning of communication is the response you get

You get what you asked for! Have you ever asked someone to do something and they have gone away and done the complete opposite? You are communicating all the time, consciously and unconsciously! If we want to achieve results then you need to be clear and concise about *all* your communication.

The map is not the territory

What you believe to be true is just *your* perception of the world. The words we use do not fully represent that item. We can change our map of the world, through changing our language and using NLP.

People make the best choices available to them

People make the best choice available to them with their current knowledge of their own resources. It may not be producing the best result for them however they have made the best choice.

There is no failure, only feedback

Ahhh, my favourite! Its feedback! Perhaps what you are doing hasn't produced the result you were after, it has however produced a certain result, just not the one you were looking for!

Rapport determines your success

The amount and level of rapport you have with someone will determine the success of your communication. If your message is not getting across then be flexible and look at the depth of the rapport. When you are aligned with someone, with good rapport, there is no resistance.

Flexibility breeds success

The person who can be most flexible in their communication can define their results. They say the first sign of insanity is doing something one way and have it not work and then doing it again, the same way, and expecting a different result! The more flexible you can be, experimenting and being curious about others and their model of the world the more successful you will be.

There are no unresourceful people only unresourceful states

NLP gives us access to the unconscious mind where most of our resources lie. We may, at times, feel unresourceful however does it mean that you have no resources? No! It just means we cannot access them at that time.

These presuppositions really assist when working with individuals and teams. To have these at the back of your mind, as part of your make up then you will be moved to a notion of curiosity and experimentation which is what NLP is all about.

Part 1
NLP experiences in real life

"What a gift a story is"
Diane MacInnes

Positive learning's

"I used the learning/spelling strategy with Jake, my son. He always struggled with spelling particularly words with more than four letters. What worked best was writing each word in different colours, breaking it down and sticking them on his bathroom mirror. He now gets all of his spellings right the majority of the time!

I was struggling with Jakes behaviour at school and he was falling behind. Jake is 5 and every day when I went to collect him from school the teacher would call me in to tell me what he had done wrong. That day it got so bad I dreaded going to school until one day I asked her if Jake ever did anything positive because all I heard were the negatives. I told her how I felt and also the fact that Jake had started saying he didn't want to go to school. All I was able to talk to him about was the negative behaviours and had nothing positive to reinforce. With regards to his progress the teacher said she believed he was capable but the teaching assistant who spent 'most' time with Jake, believed he wasn't capable and had problems with concentration. I asked the teaching assistant if her belief was having the impact that she was looking for signs that he wasn't capable and limiting his progress. We decided to log his day to day behaviour in a book broken down into morning, lunchtime and afternoon. From day one there had been significantly more positives than negatives and both Jake's behaviour and concentration have dramatically improved. So much so his end of term school report was glowing and I found it hard to believe it was about my son! The teacher assures me it is and after our meeting she reviewed her behaviour and felt guilty because the only time she spoke to parents was when something was amiss. She now consciously talks to parents about positives"

Pam Wiggins
Leeds

Techniques mentioned
Learning strategy
Mindset – positive outlook. Cause and Effect

Chuckle Knuckles

"Still not had a drop of white wine (have to sort out the red soon) but charged with this success I have challenged myself to lose weight especially after seeing some of the feedback photos from Newcastle!

* I have now lost 1st since the course
* I still have a very active "Chuckle Knuckle"
* My attitude towards everything in my life has taken on a fresh positive attitude and I thought I was already positive; but since then I stopped procrastinating over employing another consultant (He starts in 2 weeks)
* Business referrals are being attracted to me
* I read the Purple Cow and have designed a "Sneezer" product which is already selling
* I am re-writing all my course notes (with highlighted bits!) so I make the most of the stuff"

Kevin Charlton
Cheshire

Techniques used:
Anchoring
Submodalities – like to dislike
Mindset – positive action & law of attraction

Why oh why?

"I submitted a proposal to a client for a big job in a company doing coaching and training. I laid out the proposal in the way in which I thought explained all the details, costs and timelines. I had a conversation with the sponsor and he sounded confused. My message wasn't getting across the way I desired. According to what?
I then redid the proposal and presented using the 4 Mat system. He raved, took notes and accepted the price! And – I won the proposal!

Also, I worked with my nephew in relation to his exams and what he wanted to do following school. We met for a few sessions and we worked on Time Line Therapy™ – clearing negative emotions and limiting decisions. We also worked on learning strategies and the learning state. On our first session, he commented that he would get bored as he got bored after about 10 minutes. After 2 and a half hours he was dumbfounded to how long we had been working! What a result!

Altogether we worked on the above and visualisation of outcomes, creating choices, strategies for learning with visualisation. Grades for his GCSEs were predicted as 7 Es. He achieved 3 D's, 1 C, 1 DD and 1 E!!!! He is now in a course relating to performing music rather than the building course that he was going to do based on having no qualifications!

I have had great success with clients in performing personal breakthrough sessions. My very first one was with a Director of a company – we used Time Line therapy™ to release limiting decision and he has had increased confidence ever since, linking back to an incident when he was 12!

I have also reaped the rewards for myself. Using all the techniques I have overcome negative emotions, have set and achieved my outcomes. I frequently use Self hypnosis which keeps me in touch with my unconscious mind and always focus on Cause and Effect.

I use metaphors with my son Ben and focus on beliefs and an "I can attitude" with my eldest son Conor.

Within my role as a trainer, I have noticed the benefits of using multiple embedded metaphors within my training courses.

One particular course that I train/facilitate, the feedback with a certain exercise kept throwing up questions and confusion.

After my master practitioner I used opening metaphors and had no questions, higher scores on feedback! Result!"

Damian Culhane
Essex

Techniques mentioned
4mat system
Learning strategies
Learning state
Metaphors
Mindset – Cause and Effect, focus, belief
Time Line Therapy™

"Move over Tiger!"

"Hi Ailie

Please find attached my golfing score card from today which records the goal you helped me set on the Time Line Therapy™ course. To play the course 10 under using my handicap. I know we put it into September but this just lets me work on some of my other goals. I would like to thank you for the immense sense of achievement and happiness this has given me today "IT WORKS".

It's amazing how it affects your playing partner who started using words like "bandit, where's your sombrero". Once again thank you..

Michael"

**Michael Gallagher
Melrose**

*Technique used:
Time Line Therapy™ setting outcomes*

Storming the flat!

"My boyfriend was in the middle of studying for and sitting his final exams for his Masters in Law and had been somewhat agitated recently, panicking, and unable to settle down to study as he needed to.

So (having put up with quite enough pacing and harrumphing around the place) I decided to help him by doing some chaining anchors work with him, to move him to motivation. Being at the end of his tether and very morose, he was happy with the idea.

We worked out the states and examples he needed to move him away from procrastination and through to motivation. He was VERY good at procrastination, so I needed to only anchor it once!

Anyway – the chain led us through to motivation, and his strongest example of motivation was a time he went paint-balling. He loves paint-balling, is a big computer game fan, and used to be in the national rifle team when he was younger. He's also a fencer and has studied courses in stage fighting. So overall, his ideal job would be in the army apart from the fact that he wouldn't want to kill anyone!

I was so good at getting him into a motivated state; he then proceeded to give me a 20 minute lesson in the correct procedure during paint-balling (or warfare!) on how to storm a building whilst working as a team. He used a roll of cling-film as his 'gun', I had the tin foil. We stormed our flat, moving as one down the hall, into the bathroom, and captured the bedroom, taking no prisoners. I felt like a complete plonker, but he was so deadly serious about it I had to hide my giggles and play along (I wanted to keep him feeling motivated).

When his exams started I hoped he was going in feeling motivated rather than ready to wage war on the invigilators!

The story has a great ending...he got a distinction in his Masters degree and is now happily practising law. Heaven help those who stand in his way!"

Emma Jones
Bristol

Techniques mentioned
Anchoring – chaining anchors

An elephant, a skinny latte and a bottle of red wine

"I suppose that I did the usual. I completed my practitioner course, and wanted to go out and change the world. 'Come and see me, I'll stop you eating crisps/chocolate/bread etc.' (delete as appropriate).
Then I calmed down a little and decided to practice on my son first. Six times tables.
V>A>K
And he has never looked back.

Wow this stuff really works.

So................
I'm sitting under a beach brolly on holiday, and I start chatting to the woman next to me. The usual holiday stuff. This poor lady *so* wanted to join her husband when he went snorkelling but she always panicked. She knew that she would, even though she told herself not to.
'Y'know' I said 'the brain can't process a negative'. And we spent the next two hours discussing her life, her confidence and why everything went wrong. It was really moving, the lady shed a few tears, and she held my hand. She later told me that the same evening, she 'skipped into the restaurant at dinner'. The next day we chatted for a while (I should be charging, I thought. Kirsty told me there had to be a value). At the end of the holiday she bought me a wooden elephant (not her fault, we were in

Kenya there wasn't much else available) and told me I'd changed her life. I felt amazing.

Wow this stuff really works.

I'm back at work, and looking for ways to implement my new found skills. I soon realise I shouldn't be looking. The opportunities to use this are around me every single second. How do I build a better relationship? Influence others? Be a better communicator?
Easy.
I observe and I listen. And I respect the other person's model of the world.
I'm more tolerant and patient. I work really well with my boss, I just draw him diagrams (he's VERY visual).
And I'm enjoying working with people on their development. I can see a real difference. Two people at work will swear that they only got their new jobs because of the work I did with them. I'm busy changing focus, working through the keys to an achievable outcome, identifying goals, building confidence and even getting to do some 'proper' Time Line work (fantastic, so interesting!). My reputation is building and at the moment I have seven people 'on my books'. Soon I won't have time to do

my paid job! And the really great thing is............... I'm helping these people, good for them.................... but it so makes me feel great too! I'm also one wooden elephant, one bouquet of flowers, a skinny latte and one bottle of red wine better off. Wow this stuff *really* works!"

Julie Evers
Leeds

Techniques mentioned:
Learning strategy
Language – negatives, representational systems

Made from Girders

"I wanted to give up Irn Bru and Pepsi, both of which I drank far too much of.

I did Pepsi first by changing submodalities. I used saltwater to swap the Pepsi with. Someone brought a can of Pepsi over from the bar and I couldn't bring myself to drink it much as I tried.

Later I did the same with Irn Bru, this time swapping it with vomit (nice, I know!). Needless to say I haven't touched Irn Bru since (well over a year); I don't even look at it in the shops. I used to drink a 2 litre bottle a day...

Anyway, a couple of weeks after I'd done this I was at the cinema and ordered my usual popcorn and Pepsi. I was sitting in the cinema and took a big gulp of my Pepsi and thought to myself that it was off or something because it tasted foul. I took a few more sips and couldn't quite work out why it tasted so awful. I was about to take it back when I remembered what I'd done.... "

Hilary Thain
Glasgow

Techniques used:
Submodalities like to dislike

To hoe or not to hoe

"Having used Life Coaching and Motivational Coaching successfully for many years I am still surprised at the fantastic results that can be achieved using NLP techniques.

My opinion is that any process can be best judged by the effect it has on you personally, both emotionally and physically. In other words, try before you buy. I used to have the same opinion of any kind of chocolate. Not anymore – liked to disliked away by Kirsty. My mouth still jack-knifes at the sight of a milky bar.

After the initial success I thought it might be an idea to deal with some of my limiting beliefs – the ones that even as a coach you have difficulty shifting. Quick float down the timeline, provisional licence in the post. And my fear of getting behind the wheel and causing devastation to both the flora and fauna of my local habitat. All gone thanks again to Kirsty. It would be a shame to stop there.

Procrastination.

My garden is now almost completed and 'to hoe or not to hoe' is no longer a question for the weekend (I wonder if she has a technique for peonies envy).

I could go on but my remit was for a short piece- and I have just accidentally rubbed my chuckle knuckle and I am unable to giggle and write simultaneously. Suffice to say, I have been swished along my timeline and had my anchors well and truly collapsed in all the right places. I wonder what's next?

And it's good to wonder...... "

Gary Anderson
Glasgow

Techniques used:
Anchoring –collapse anchors
Time Line Therapy™
Submodalities – swish pattern
Submodalities – Like to dislike
Submodalities – limiting belief change

Is it OK to be OK?

"When I look back now to see what NLP has done for me and how my life has been different, I realise that my life would have been OK if I never decided to do the training.

After all, it is ok to be in a job that I hate. It is ok to have dreams that won't ever happen. It is ok to just sit at home and not have enough energy to fully appreciate my family. It is ok not to be happy with me or other people around me.

All of this is ok because you know what; it's not my fault... or is it?

Then the following words really brought me down to earth:
'You don't necessary create all the bad things that happen to you... but... the sum total of all your choices, both conscious and unconscious choices, have led you to where you are today.'

So I made one choice, I'm not allowed to blame other people for where I am today anymore. I decided to be very honest with myself and I took a long, hard look at where I wanted my life to go.

It is now 12 months later since I started with my NLP journey and Wow, what a ride.

By using Time Line Therapy™ I got rid of all the emotions that unconsciously held me back. With NLP techniques, I re-aligned all the things I value most in my career, relationships, spirituality and health. I feel much happier now that I have taken full control of my life.

I have recently started my own company and I do now what I really want to do in life. When I'm with my wife and two kids, I don't just waste away on the couch but we actually spend quality time now. I'm in a habit of exercising and eating healthy, something my body has needed for years and it is about time I treat it with respect.

I'm not saying that I have turned into superman, some kind of wonder family man or that I won't ever fail again. I'm just saying that I have realised where the buck stops, and that I'm willing to accept the consequences of all my decisions and actions.

To me NLP is all the stuff we already know but are unconscious about. Its knowledge that turns into a lifestyle and I'm very glad that there are people like Kirsty who can reinvent NLP to give you the quality training that you deserve.
Watch this space, this is only the beginning!"

Mawgen Schoeman
Leeds

Techniques used:
Achieving outcomes – keys to an achievable outcome
Values realignment
Time Line Therapy™ – releasing negative emotions and limiting decisions
Mindset – Cause and Effect.

Fizzy sweets, cats and a whole lot of work!

"Well what a year it has been. Back in July 2006, I was busy working away in a large UK bank and had a very promising career in management ahead of me. Then I went to my 7 day NLP Practitioner Certification training and my life has changed dramatically – but for the better!!!

Since my first course, I have completed my Time Line Therapy™ and Hypnotherapy Practitioner certifications and then went onto have a fantastic 12 days in Glasgow, where I successfully achieved certification in NLP, Time Line Therapy™ and Hypnotherapy at the Master Practitioner Level. Now that was a fantastic course, as I not only had a massive personal breakthrough, I was able to work with a fellow delegate to complete a full personal breakthrough session with her successfully!!!

I had always thought that the only way that I could be successful in life, was to work hard and pursue a career in a large corporate environment!! However, part of me wanted to be free to do what I wanted and become my own boss!!! Well after a massive breakthrough, I got rid of all my negative emotions and limiting decisions and decided to go for it!!!

So I left my job to start up my own training company, to specialise in NLP, Time Line Therapy™ and Hypnotherapy, so I can continue to share the knowledge of these subjects with many others, so they can achieve success and breakthroughs in their personal and business lives.

It has been a challenging couple of months whilst setting up my business and raring to go – but I haven't looked back since – the journey to achieving the life I want has only just begun!!!

As I am writing this, I am in the middle of my latest challenge, as I am in Las Vegas completing my NLP, Time Line Therapy™ and Hypnotherapy Trainer's Certification Training, with the infamous Drs Tad and Adrianna James!! I am having such a fantastic time and learning lots. I can't wait to get back to the UK to deliver my first training course!!

If someone had told me 12 months ago that I would be where I am, I would have laughed at them, but it proves to me that if you believe in yourself and go for your big dreams, then things around you fall into place to help you get there …. If you want it enough!!!

Also, the last year has seen me get officially engaged to my fiancée Shareen, with both our families being very supportive and happy for us. We are busy planning our wedding for next summer!!!

I have also had great results with my mum, who has always had a phobia of cats, but last week I was on the phone to her and she said, 'hold on a minute .. shooo… shooo!'. I asked her what she was doing and she said, 'there was just a cat at the side door, I was just telling it to go away' in such a calm and collected way – instead of screaming and shouting like she would have previously done!!!

I also haven't ever eaten a 'fizzy sweet' since my NLP Practitioner course, since I decided to give them up!!!! That reminds me there are many other foods that I want to stop eating .... ☺

I just hope that the next year will just be as fantastic and transformational as the last".

Osmaan Sharif
Glasgow

Techniques mentioned:
Outcomes – achieving outcomes
Parts integration
Fast Phobia model
Submodalities – like to dislike change
Mindset – Cause and Effect, focus.

Fight or flight

"I had a phobia of wasps for as long as I could remember. The minute I saw a wasp or heard buzzing I would scream and leave the room. I regularly embarrassed myself when this happened in public and put myself in danger when I swerved my car when a wasp flew in. If a wasp came into my house, I would have to ring my mum to come and remove it from my house. My phobia was so bad; it would often reduce me to tears. On a scale of 1-10, I would describe my fear as 10.

On the NLP Practitioner course, Kirsty took me through the fast phobia model. I had to teach her my phobia, describing all the feelings and thoughts I experienced to her. At the end of the session, on a scale of 1-10 my fear had reduced right down to around a 2.

Even more surprising, I was able to remember the first event that triggered my phobia. I remember going on a camping trip with my family to the Isle of Anglesey, Wales, when I was about 8 years old. It was a very warm day and we were sat outside our tent having jam sandwiches. A swarm of wasps came and virtually attacked us, they were all over our food, and I almost swallowed one that had gone on my jam sandwich. I was really frightened and cried hysterically. My brother and sisters teased me and laughed at my reaction to the wasps. This was a memory that I had previously completely buried.

Since the course, I have come into contact with wasps on several occasions; the difference in me is amazing. Whilst I am not fully happy when around wasps, I can function normally and even kill them with a newspaper. This is a major breakthrough for me!!

And another thing....

For many years, I have not enjoyed flying. Whilst I will fly, I get very nervous before a flight and once on the plane have physical symptoms such as sweaty palms, feeling sick and my heart beats fast. I sit very rigidly during takeoff and only ever take off my seat belt if I am desperate to use the loo!

On the Time Line Therapy™ course, I worked with a partner on my fear of flying. When going back to the first event that caused this fear, I realised it was the first time I flew which was at Christmas when I was 16 and on a school trip skiing to Switzerland. I was very excited about the trip but the flight was not good. There was a lot of turbulence, the plane looked old and shook a lot. I was terrified, even more so because I was travelling without my family. Throughout the whole skiing trip, I did not enjoy myself; I was very homesick and fearful of the flight home. After the trip, I told everyone I had a brilliant time as it was not cool at 16 be homesick and miss your mum. I definitely did not want to go away again without them. I developed a fear of flying so I had an excuse not to go away again.

The session made me realise that I did not have a real fear of flying, it was just a strategy I had developed when I was 16 to cover up being homesick and not wanting to travel without my family, however, over the years I taught myself to fear flying.

I can't wait now for my next holiday in September to see if uncovering this memory makes a difference to how I react on the flight!!"

Karen McGowan
Leeds

Techniques used:
Fast Phobia model
Time Line Therapy™

Successful successes

"What a blast that week was. The course has changed my life and I'm notching up the successes already. They may not seem very big to you but they're HUGE in my model of the world. Here's a few to start:

RON SUCCESS 1

Tanya and I share the joy of having twins. When we worked with each other on 'collapsing anchors', we also shared the desire to overcome getting irritated by the little darlings. For me it was their continually asking 'but why, Daddy?' which would eventually get me 'somewhat upset'.

I had lunch with my kids on Sunday and heard my son (13, going on 33) say 'why' once too much. But instead of getting irritated by it I looked at him and said 'are you really interested in knowing or are you just winding me up?' He blushed bright red, smiled and said 'maybe a bit of both'. And we both had a good laugh about it. Success!

RON SUCCESS 2

Our next door neighbours are away on holiday, but I could never help my partner to help feed and clean out the kids' rabbit and hamsters – the latter were two 'rat-like' for me. Sunday morning I helped her clean them all out. I handled the rabbit, admittedly, while she did the hamsters. But I was with them, which is a success for me. Maybe I can do the hamsters tomorrow.

RON SUCCESS 3

Johnny and Karen helped me do a Swish on being able to walk up to my MD's office when I arrived at work each morning to say hello (rather than just sitting down at my desk and not risk any possible rejection). This morning (Monday) I confidently strode past my desk and went straight to my MD's office to say hello, just as I'd pictured it – but he wasn't there! (Later found out that he's on leave this week.) But I carried on and said good morning to everyone else who was in. They all seem pleased, nobody rejected me in any way and it felt good.

RON SUCCESS 4

My 'limiting belief' was that I could never contemplate working on my own, as an independent consultant. But last night I started (for the first time) discussing with my partner the practicalities of doing so. It's nice to at least have that choice available to me now."

Ron Symington
Hertfordshire

Techniques mentioned:
Anchoring – collapse anchors
Fast Phobia model (for rats phobia)
Submodalities – swish pattern
Submodalities – belief change

Educating Education

"My friend Julia and I decided to do the NLP practitioner training course in Spring 2006. It was initially completely for personal reasons for us both. We had both been intrigued when we first heard about NLP & were dying to find out more. We thought we'd never really be able to get the chance to do so because the courses were 1 week long and we were both teachers.

But of course as luck would have it (or should I say the law of attraction would have it) we found a course that was running during that particular Easter holidays and so we signed up!!

We both had a very inspiring week with lots of light bulb moments, mini breakthroughs and great re-affirmations of previous beliefs about abilities and our thinking. It wasn't until we got back to the classroom that we realised what an absolute fantastic tool NLP was in schools and the wonders it can achieve with children.

We are both Head of Years in a comprehensive secondary school and I can't tell you how easily we fall into 'rapport' now with all our pupils (and even the parents!). NLP has hugely benefited our teaching and our leadership skills. Every assembly we do now has an NLP presupposition theme!!

Our whole thinking and approach to pupils has changed for the better and it has brought even more enjoyment to our careers.

We realised we had something special here and something that needed to be shared with other teachers, trainee teachers and pupils. And so…….an idea was born. The following year we had completed the Master Practitioner course and set up a company in order to bring NLP into education. And so that's exactly what we're doing! Teachers are so receptive and understand modelling excellence and teaching pupils how to get the most out of their minds is just so important. We're still teaching of course, because that's our passion and we feel it's so important that trainers in education are continuously aware of what goes on in 'working' schools.

Whenever a pupil says 'Miss I can't do it?' Just reply, 'And what would happen if you could?' Before you know it the pupil has visualised the solution and your work is done!

NLP has brought our enthusiasm for teaching and promising new career possibilities to new heights. It's amazing how life's little twists and turns bring you places you never even dreamed of!! The world is a weird and wonderful place and NLP makes it all achievable!!"

Clair Donegan & Julia Armstrong
London

Techniques used:
Presuppositions of NLP
Mindset – Cause and Effect
Outcomes

What procrastination?

"Just a wee note to say I have done two runs already (short ones but never the less!) I haven't procrastinated once; ironing done, back garden tidied, bicycle brought out of storage and checked - one long bike ride with kids undertaken (can hardly sit down but was good!) with promise of at least one long bike excursion per week...

On the work front my mind set is so different ...my RAS is in gear and I have even taken the bold step of offering my services to a lady who has a phobia of lifts (by the way Catharine how are you doing?) I am off to see her to discuss it next week - took a lot of nerve and was a bit scared of rejection but I remembered Tad saying collect the "no's so went for it, she seems really pleased that I may be able to help.

The kids both have chuckle knuckles. I have been trying to apply one to the hubby... while he has been asleep!!! HA!!! Never mind will convert him in the end...

Must admit he was impressed by the fast phobia model on my son's fear of oranges...20 minutes and he was holding one in his hand (something that he would NEVER have contemplated before, in fact he wouldn't even stay in the same room as an orange before!) the best thing about it was how pleased he looked with himself afterwards, he kept saying "I feel really good about myself now" - great or what!

Thank you so much everyone for a fabulous week,
XXX"

Christine Mclean
Leeds

Techniques mentioned:
Anchoring – chaining anchors
Anchoring – basic anchors (chuckle knuckles!)
Fast phobia model

Hello up there!

"Up until August this year I had a fear of heights. I hadn't always had it, it was one of those that had popped up with age and was about as wanted as the wrinkles appear with age almost as randomly!

On the NLP Practitioner Course we talked about the Fast Phobia model and Kirsty used this to work with me on getting rid of my fear of heights. At the time there were no tall building or hills about to test if it had worked... so these pictures are me testing it out in September in the Lake District - what better place?!

The first one is Go-Ape - lots of tall trees and ropes, the last two are the top of the Old Man of Coniston, 803 metres up. I'm the one in black & white on the right. The Old Man was a 3 hour climb up and so I had plenty of time to get scared, it just didn't happen.

The phobia model only took about 15 minutes and was fantastic fun to do, the latter part being very unexpected!"

Penny Bedford
York

Techniques used:
Fast Phobia Model

Because we can you know.

"Thank you so much for the most amazing week of my life - I've been reborn and am seeing the world through new eyes. Can't tell you how much I'm enjoying the puzzled looks around me here at work, but there are lots of smiles coming my way. I can feel the energy around me and it's so huge everyone else feels it too. How fantastic is that!

I've signed up my first client - my brother. Saw him yesterday and knew he'd be up for it. Previously I wouldn't have expected this response but I put it out there and had absolutely no doubt of the outcome.

When I set out for work this morning, I recalled you and all my Practitioner chums from last week and felt so cheerful and alive when I walked through the office beaming at everyone. Daphne and Hyacinth are popping up all over the place, bless them, and I'm so delighted to have them with me.

Have a fantastic week."

Janet Courtenay
Preston

Techniques mentioned:
Mindset – positive focus
Anchoring

Mum's the word

"Hi everyone - it's Monday night and I think I have finally 'come back into the room'!! What an absolutely life changing week - and I want to thank all of you for making it so brilliant. It was a real honour working with you all and seeing all the positive stuff happening in all of us.

Well - success already for me. Having been away all week my boys have reacted, now that I'm back in the only way they know i.e. loads of fighting and attention seeking from me.........and I felt really weird - it was as if my normal irritation which I would have felt had just gone, and my husband commented on how calm I seem to be with them now! It's such a relief - it's a bit like poking an abscess, waiting for the pain, then when there is none you can just get on with living again! Excellent!!

Had a meeting this morning with the guy who's advising me on the website for my new business, and I did all the rapport and it felt much more natural now!"

Anon
Manchester

Techniques mentioned:
Anchoring – collapse anchors
Mindset – focus, Cause and Effect

I mean business...

"Well since I last wrote (AGES) ago I watched the Secret as you advised, bought the book and the audio CDs and have practiced and practiced like MAD!

And this Monday just gone, I handed my notice in at work (millions of years in the NHS and now going self employed starting in Oct), I have three contracts for training and service improvement work which will take me to December and I feel FANTASTIC!!!!!

The thing that's kept me going is remembering you saying, at the NLP training in Leeds when I asked how work was going you said "Oh this isn't work, it's play" and I thought "I want to be able to say that" and soon I will be able to...wow!
Just set up bank account and going to ring accountant next week, it's all so exciting....

So Kirst...any more advice would be more than welcome as your last little tip worked wonders!

Hope you are fantastic
Take care
Love
ChrisXXX
PS CMc Consulting (oooo errr missus!!)

Christine McLean
Leeds

Techniques mentioned
Outcomes – setting achievable outcomes
Mindset – focus, choices

Radio calling!

"Hi Kirsty, I just had to write and tell you my news – what a day! I was at home this morning thinking about ringing you – had a cuppa sat down with the phone and then it rang. It was a woman from BBC Radio Sheffield asking me if I'd be happy to go on the radio live at 12.40 to talk about habits – what they are, how we develop them and how we can break them!

Bugger me I thought and whilst my mind was screaming NO NO NO my voice said yes and that was that. I had George so had to race him across the park to my friend's house and dump him there in time to get back and do the interview by phone. It was amazing – I was so nervous, no actually terrified and when the interview started it was bloody brilliant.

I really enjoyed it and forgot about being on live radio. Interestingly, when I got home from dropping G off, I did some prep – just a mind map as a memory jogger and I never even referred to it, it just all came naturally. Talk about a high – I had a new client tonight and that went brilliantly too, so I'm high as a kite at the moment and simply had to share it with someone who would understand how I'm feeling.

So, I have!

Hope your day has been totally fabulous and I will call you tomorrow – expect a giddy Sheffield lass on the end of your phone line!

Nitey-night, sleep tight
Xxx

Ps the icing on the cake, when I picked G up after the interview, they'd listened to it and he came running up to me going "Mummy, I've just heard you on the radio – it was cool"!!!!

Jude Eller
Sheffield

For the record – this is a monumental result for Jude. On her first course, Jude was petrified about speaking in public and we worked on anchors together and she has gone from strength to strength!

Techniques mentioned:
Anchoring – resource anchors
Mindset - belief

"I want to sort my sh*t out!"

"Those are the words I used to 'express' how I was feeling, classy eh!
The journey started with a 'Meta Model' session of let's get specific! This brought up my black-bags that had been pushed down for so long………. I knew I had crumbled, those around me knew too and I realised it was time to get help! For some individuals reading this, you might relate to this one, help, isn't something I easily ask for!

Essential to me was having the safe environment, the quality of expertise I would receive and the post support…….. Not much then!

Through the experience of Time Line Therapy™ and the trust I felt in the therapist, I was able to detach those emotions that I'd allow to suppress me in my every-day life. Once I was aware of what they were and their impact, boy did I want rid! I knew my life was good in parts but I believed I could feel better, a happiness. For me, the real treasure is the 'learning's' you glean.

After my TLT session, exhaustion and dehydration overwhelmed together with a quiet sense of calm. That night I slept like a baby and over the next couple of days, inner peace starting to take hold.

So what's happened since then ………………… In a nutshell a lot!

I know my journey is continuous and as I write this, I know there's much more to learn though the progress already has been significant, so here goes;

I feel happy and content! Sounds simple I know!

I've now developed the habit of asking myself what I've learnt from the different events and ensure I see those 'learns' as knowledge and gifts.

Ability to let go of people and situations that aren't healthy, example of this is cutting the 'cord' of a recent partnership that was limiting in trust, support and love – the relief tells me it was the right thing to do!

I can still wake tired and grumpy but 'eck' it's me who determines my day ...... doesn't take me long to get into a good place and enjoy it.   Guess what, I seem to meet so many enthusiastic like-minded people nowadays!

I can do whatever I want.... sounds scary and exciting at the same time.

My desire to learn has been increased and this has been evident in both work and home.

My relationships with friends and work colleagues has become much deeper through communication and understanding.

I live the presuppositions – to me they are 'empowering beliefs'.

My auditory sense has been increased – guess this is through listening to the 20 Tad cd's!

Visualise the 'greatness' of an experience!
I remove myself from individuals/situations that I believe are negative – my senses have been heightened and my removal skills are second to none now! Those individuals/situations don't serve us!

If I had to summarise;
It's not the material things that make you truly happy, for me it's my inner-peace and I recognise this must be nurtured now and in the future.
I now get asked, 'why are you so happy'?! Need I say more, apart from thank-you! "

Tracey Underwood
Leeds
Techniques mentioned:
Language - Meta Model – specific questioning tools
Presuppositions of NLP
Time Line Therapy™
Values
Mindset – cause and effect, focus.

Bed, breakfast and life coaching

"Where I am TODAY and what I expect to do in the future is influenced to a large degree by the practical application of NLP skills and the Law of Attraction on a daily basis. My future successes are every bit as real for me as the here and now - if not, more so...

My search for the route to a more successful way of living.
It started as a very personal spiritual quest in my walk with God. I was increasingly becoming convinced of the power of right thinking and focusing on what was desired as opposed to giving weight to the immediacy of negative circumstances.

While attending an NLP practitioner course in Glasgow we were shown The Secret video. To say it got me a little excited was to say the least - an understatement. It highlighted a lot of the principles I had been getting as growing revelation in my life over a matter of months and which I was just beginning to put into play.

What especially struck me was the fact that the SECRET has never really been a secret and its power (which I choose to call one of God's universal laws) is freely available to those who follow three specific steps:

1. An intense desire for the knowledge of how to excel in living

2. The conviction to actually put it into practice

And finally

3. The strength of belief to be persistent UNTIL the manifestation comes

As you are reading this book I can assume you may at least have some degree of desire. My prayer is that you will engage with the other 2 steps and be fully appreciative of such wonderful opportunity that the divine allows.

Carol Monteith
Inverness

Techniques mentioned:
Focus, outcomes, the law of attraction

It's a small world!

"At my NLP Practitioners course we set our goals into our time line and were reassured that the 'how' was not ours to worry about, just the what;

I set my goal. By February 12th 2008 I will be able to hold a conversation in Icelandic. All I had to do now was believe it.

A month ago I was paying a cheque in at the post office………. one of those little shabby things at the back of a local shop just around the corner from work.

I was in a great mood, the sun was shining and there was nobody queued.

'Wow what a great tan' I said to the cashier. 'It's only a gardeners tan' she laughed, 'that and she's just spent two weeks in Iceland and the weather was amazing' grumbled her colleague.

'Amazing' I cooed 'I love Iceland'……….. Where did you go?
'Reykjavik' she said, 'my mum's from Iceland so I go and stay with relatives.'

'Oh my God, do you speak Icelandic?' I squealed.

'Yes!'

'I am learning and its sooo tricky………. '

'We should meet up and maybe I could help you.'

How the heck did that happen?……….. Oh yes, I set my goal and the law of attraction sorted it for me. ☺

Vith syowmst, verteu blesseuth (*I'll see you, be blessed*) a typical Icelandic goodbye."

Erica x

Erica Course
Hampshire

Techniques used:
Law of attraction and outcomes

All aboard!

"I think there are three precious things I took from NLP
- I am driving the bus!!! No one makes me angry I make me angry in fact I make myself feel however I choose!!!.
- 2 of my friends attended the course on my recommendation and it was great to see the benefits
- I was soooooo scared of spiders. After a swish pattern I am now in control of my fear. I stayed in the jungle for 2 nights in Sri Lanka recently; I would never have even contemplated this for fear of seeing a big spider. It was a big achievement for me."

Carol Harte
Leeds

Techniques used:
Presuppositions
Fast phobia model
Mindset – Cause and Effect

Upgrading life

"Thanks for the lovely week of NLP.
I am home and happily spreading the word of NLP. My trip coming back was very eventful with my newly learnt technique of rapport.

I was flying by British Airways and I genuinely thought this air pursor was having good personality and could see his good energy.

I instantly told him and complimented to him about what I felt, (used rapport). Later I asked him for a red label whisky (small bottle) I told him I wanted to carry it with me as I was spending 6 hrs in Heathrow before my next flight.

He went in and got me a bagful of whiskies, wow that was some rapport, my first gift of rapport building.

My next strategy was to check in without paying for my excess luggage so I had to get in rapport with the girl at the counter who checks my luggage in.

I first got into rapport with a fellow passenger, later told him about my excess luggage and used some presuppositions to convince him to adjust his luggage weight with mine as he was travelling light, and then told the girl on the counter, that she was the star of the day and the most important person in my life as she told me the excess weight was 56 kgs, all the rapport building with the fellow passenger and the counter girl helped me checking my luggage for free, thanks to rapport.

Wow it doesn't end here!

I wanted an aisle seat and I got it too, with my friends help, of course a new friend, the flight pursor.

I felt all were my targets for the day to achieve what I wanted, and got it, I got the seat too which I marked in my mind.

Thanks for the power, the power of the mind
Thanks Kirsty"

Rahul Patil
Mumbai

Techniques mentioned:
Rapport

The Visioning - Anchoring Continuum!!

"Some time ago, when I was with a previous organisation, the organisation was taken over by a competitor. As a result hundreds of people were to be made redundant throughout the global organisation. I was one of them.

Shortly after the take-over the new organisation decided to have a global meeting in Madrid for the top 400 executives that would be part of this new organisation. This was not to include me!

However prior to the takeover I was part of a global team working on executive and organisation development. My then boss asked me that although I was to be made redundant the week following the Madrid meeting would I be willing to go to the meeting as a 'Facilitator.' I agreed!

Now at the plenary session of the meeting three groups who had been working on various aspects of building the new post take-over business had to present to the CEO and the Executive Committee. I had worked with one of these teams and had 'prepared' one of the senior delegates to present for 20 minutes on the group's recommendations. At the last minute he pulled out! After discussion with the group they asked that I make the presentation.

And here comes the visualisation bit. Although I had worked to prepare the other executive I had not really geared myself up to make this presentation. However I felt that despite my pending redundancy if I made a WOW delivery other options may open up for me. Following on some visualisation work I had done on the NLP workshop I pictured myself in the conference hall, giving an animated and impactful presentation so vividly that I could hear myself and feel the adrenalin rush. I even visualised my conclusion ending with a standing ovation!! And this was a serious business presentation to 400 seasoned execs! I pictured this scene over and over again and saw and heard myself deliver way and above what I would have expected to deliver.

In the end - I got my standing ovation. Shortly after the Chief Executive - who I had never met - approached me and asked what my role was in the new organisation. When I told him I was leaving next week he said 'not likely!' In the event I was offered a new position and stayed with the organisation for a further 5 years!

And the link to anchoring?

Well every time I have to make a presentation I recall that performance!
I relive it and see what I saw then, hear myself and hear the standing ovation. I also conjure up the feelings I had at that moment. I anchor it by clenching my fist and repeating 'Yes, Yes

Yes' to myself. I carry on doing this as I get ready to present. And guess what - even in the most tense of situations I receive tremendous feedback about the quality of the presentation.

What's more I work with others to help them present way beyond their expectations by using this technique - and they do!!"

David Kelly
Bexhill-on-sea

Techniques used:
Anchoring

Wobblegob and weight loss

"Well, where do I start?
NLP and the Law of Attraction! It definitely is a gift, I have gained so much from it both personally and professionally. Personally I haven't eaten chocolate or crisps for about 18 months and have lost nearly 2 stone (fantastic !!). I have lost wobblegob (thanks Kirsty!).

I have dived into a pool, swam underwater and most importantly got my hair wet, which had never happened in the previous 42 years!

After having my own personal breakthrough session on Master Practitioner (Thanks Rosie), I now feel me, I enjoy being me and now know to concentrate on the things I do want and find it so much easier to be positive. I really have learnt positively from the past and really enjoy the now and "my future is bright" (the future is orange – are we allowed to advertise?)

Time Line Therapy™ is amazing and so quick!
As a family we have definitely benefited. (I won't embarrass them with anecdotes as I have just remembered this is going to be printed).

Professionally, if you had told me a few years ago, I would be running my own business, I would have laughed.

The law of attraction definitely played a part in it. I only mentioned to my personal trainer (Katie) that I was thinking about finding a room and the next thing I knew I had a contract for the room and reclining chair ,a company name , a website a business account, business cards and a suit !!

I have met so many amazing people both as clients and on the courses. With clients it is wonderful to see people transform in such a short time. It is very rewarding to see the difference that people can make by releasing the negativity from the past, regaining control and having goals for the future!

The other people on all the courses were absolutely amazing. It is brilliant to meet people from all walks of life and really get on. The humour on Master Practitioner was amazing and breaking the board is definitely a life changing moment.

It is so easy to be positive with clients as I know personally that NLP and the law of attraction works!!!"

Colette Boyden
Sheffield

Techniques mentioned:
Submodalities – swish pattern
Submodalities – like to dislike
Fast phobia model
Outcomes – keys to an achievable outcome
Time Line Therapy™

The Jobs yours!

"My confidence was at an all time high recently when I was head hunted by someone I worked with for only a short period of time. New challenge, new company and a reasonable wage rise without trying, just positive thoughts!!! I accepted verbally then realized that the way it was being done was not sitting with me comfortably, it didn't feel right.

My current manager talked and talked and tried to persuade me to stay, more money, more responsibility, work the hours I wanted etc etc. I took a few days to think about it, one hat on thinking about how would I feel if I went with the other job and one hat on thinking about how would I feel if I stayed. Morally the hat fitted better in the job I was in. I decided to withdraw my verbal job acceptance with the other company and was told to call anytime if I changed my mind in the future. I now have over 10% of a wage rise with an annual bonus and some new challenges in my role.

The law of attraction helped me through this time, staying positive comfortable with the outcome."

Anon

Techniques mentioned:
Law of Attraction

Using your loaf

"I started working in a bakery when I was 14 years old, enjoying the taste and smell of newly baked bread. After 15 years in the bakery trade I changed jobs to work in the finance world/ Thought there would be more dough!

I continued to eat a lot of bread with most meals. When I was 40 years old I was diagnosed with arthritis in my hands. One of the tests showed intolerance to gluten found in wheat and yeast which are ingredients in bread.

For 4 years I struggled to give up bread. In the meantime I had set up my own Training and Development Company; this is when I discovered the use of NLP.

When attending the NLP practitioner's course one of the sessions was moving likes to dislikes. This was an opportunity to test this against my love of bread. Kevin who was also a student on the course started to get me to picture sliced bread then I pictured my dislike which was slices of lamb. I have never been able to eat lamb.

We completed the exercise and went home that evening. In the morning in my usual habit of putting 2 slices of bread in the toaster, I just stopped before putting them in saying to myself that I did not want this bread.

Also at the end of course dinner the rest of the students thought it was funny watching me try to eat my soup avoiding the croutons. And that was March 2007, I had never eaten a piece of bread until the end of July when I tried a slice but it tasted disgusting and I am still bread free to this day, thanks to Kevin and NLP."

Michael Gallagher.
Melrose

Techniques used:
Submodalities like to dislike

Shine a light

"I have a lovely, vibrant, warm, funny and smart client, and she's truly inspirational to me. I feel blessed to work with her and I just want to tell you about one occasion, during a very challenging time for her personally, when she was finding it difficult to cope and felt there was no clarity in her life now or for the future.

She told me she had a naughty and mischievous imp inside her head, laughing at her and telling her "Ha, you thought you'd started to sort things out didn't you; well you haven't. You can't make everything ok". She went on to say although this was clearly the voice of the imp, it felt like a ball of wool was inside her head, originating in her temples – in her words she felt she was going mad. I thought about the way she'd described this to me and the words she used. For me, it appeared to be a part of her that was asking her (in an unhelpful way) to slow down a bit, take things steady and reflect a bit more on the amazing progress she was making in her life, and it therefore had honourable intentions and was simply going about things the wrong way. Instead of slowing down a bit, she had become sad, confused and cried – a lot.

We did a belief change using submodalities to shift her from her belief that this 'imp' didn't want her to have a nice relaxed life, to an angel that supported her, reminded her of her inner strength and courage, and loved her. After we'd finished, she told me she felt 'trancey and spaced out – chilled and a bit tired' so we ended there.

When we spoke the following week, she told me a story about how she'd been at her parent's house, sitting in the sun and gazing up at the sky. She noticed a pink shaded light through the clouds and 'felt' her angel. At that moment, Nicola named her angel Rose, as the pink in the sky reminded her of rosehips and she remembered reading a book about a Rosehip Fairy. Rose now guides Nicola, not in a sense of advising her what to do, but simply by being there with her, loving her and trusting her judgement; allowing her feelings of warmth, peace, security and happiness.

During our remaining sessions, we laughed a lot and I learned a wonderful thing from this experience. It was as though she almost gave me permission to enjoy my work, to face my fears and insecurities head on and deal with them, to try new things and trust my judgement, and I'll always be grateful to her for sharing her story with me, trusting me and giving me the opportunity to grow as a practitioner and a human. We email each other quite regularly even though our work for the moment is done. It's always a pleasure to see her name pop up in my inbox – how many jobs or lines of work do you get this from I wonder? My favourite quote of all time comes from Nelson Mandela's inaugural speech. I always found it inspirational and compelling, and through working with this fantastic woman, I experienced the essence of it for myself – a true gift.

"Our deepest fear is not that we are inadequate. Our deepest fear is that we are powerful beyond measure. It is our light, not our darkness that frightens us. We ask ourselves who am I to be brilliant, gorgeous, talented and fabulous? Actually, who are you not to be? Your playing small doesn't serve the world. There is nothing enlightened about shrinking so that others won't feel insecure around you. As we let our own light shine, we consciously give other people permission to do the same. As we are liberated from our own fear, our presence automatically liberates others.
Nelson Mandela – Inaugural speech 1994"

Jude Eller
Sheffield

Techniques mentioned:
Parts integration
Submodalities – belief change

The outcome of goal setting

"After completing my NLP Practitioner with Kirsty I was wowed with all the new techniques I had learned for my own personal development. On the course Kirsty asked near the beginning why we were on the course and how she said it may change by the end of it. To be honest I never understood the powerful changes it could make in a therapeutic and coaching of an individual.

After the course I realised I wanted to develop a career on helping people achieve their goals and let go of the barriers that had held them back.

On returning to work people asked how the course went, life changing was the answer I gave them. I told people what it was about and how it could change people's lives within a few sessions. At work Lucy (not her real name) was a girl on the reception desk she was very capable, had a degree and wanted to progress in the leisure industry. On one of my days off Lucy had been mugged at gun point in Manchester. This resulted in Lucy having time off work and affected her emotionally. She struggled to go to the car in the morning and shopping was not an option. Lucy approached me at work and said she understood I could help with problems and would I be able to meet with her.

I had my NLP skills and was due to start a Time Line Therapy™ course in a few weeks which I knew was powerful in letting go of negative emotions. I agreed to work with Lucy, over two sessions I followed the detailed personal history, anchoring, swish patterns Time Line Therapy™ and the fast phobia model. At times there were tears and then I knew I had got somewhere then Lucy started to laugh about the whole situation. Lucy was amazed by how she had got her life back; she got a promotion at work and is back to her old self.

An hour after the last session I got a text from Lucy saying she was going shopping at the weekend and thanks for everything.

I am now in the process of setting up Breakthrough Sessions at the Gym I work in all in just over a year since I searched on the internet and stumbled across NLP and thought wow that sounds interesting!"

Mark Thompson
Yorkshire

Techniques used:
Outcomes – keys to an achievable outcome
Fast phobia model
Time Line Therapy™

Reporting Dyslexia

"Dyslexia - Can reducing dyslexia really be this easy?

I met a delightful client recently, KT, aged 17, who had been diagnosed as dyslexic at around 12 years old. I dislike labels so I asked her what she would she like to be able to do better.

Typical comments from her school reports listed weak comprehension skills, poor short term memory and difficulty with spelling. She had to read sentences four or five times before she understood their meaning or had any chance of remembering what she read. KT had previously tried the DAT and the "Toe by Toe" repetitive techniques. DAT appeared to improve her balance but neither had been very helpful for reading, understanding and recall. (In exams KT had been supported by a scribe and a reader for difficult words.)

KT's dream was to become a primary school teacher, but she was painfully close to losing that dream as nobody, in her teacher's words, "who would want a teacher for their child who spelt so poorly". We discussed her artistic abilities. She could draw an object in front of her and had produced some vibrant modern art but found drawing or painting anything from memory, such as a field of cows quite impossible. KT had progressed reasonably well in mathematics. Mental arithmetic, however, was a complete "no go" area. She was studying English at advanced level. Her balance improved when she was taught not to look at her feet but to look up. Similarly, when driving, one needs to look at the road ahead, rather than at the bonnet. In addition, her habit of looking at her feet meant that KT was more likely to be "in her feelings" – no doubt running an internal dialogue about how poor her balance was and how difficult it was to walk.

After just two hours practising *Seeing Spells Achieving* techniques, KT had mastered visual spelling. She could spell words like dinosaur, dyslexic and gorgeous both forwards and backwards. She learnt how to visualise stories so that she would be able to remember them, successfully complete a comprehension exercise, and remember lists of shopping and so on. And should she wish to paint scenes from memory, KT would also be able to draw on her visual memory. She also realised that she could write without looking down at the paper - an invaluable skill when you have notes or homework to copy down from a blackboard.

Whenever KT successfully visualised a word she laughed out loud and the entire session was tremendous FUN. She is now looking forward with far more confidence to a career as a teacher or special needs co-ordinator. – And has experienced for herself some of the many benefits of mastering the *Seeing Spells Achieving* visualisation skills. With a grin from ear to ear KT declared: "This is so easy, no longer the hard work it used to be for me".

Olive Hickmott
Techniques used:
Learning strategies
Visualisation

How not to get sick

"Life 'hints' at us all the time, whether it throws opportunity our way or just nudges to where we should be but so often we are too caught up in now to realise what's in front of us; and that's when life brings out the big guns!!

Being sick is never a good experience whether it's a little cold or something more serious. For me being ill over the last 9 months was life 'bringing out the big guns' simply because I could not see what was right there in front of me.

I have worked in the hair and beauty industry for 17 years and own a successful salon in Edinburgh. I love my work and enjoy the interaction of meeting new people every day although dealing with people can be tiring and dealing with employees even more so. It seemed reasonable to me to work 16 hour days, every day, and to have a home life and hobbies and everything else you can cram into those little 24 hours that squeeze into a day.

I became ill with a glandular fever type virus and allowed it to really get hold because I COULD NOT take the time off work to recover. So when I eventually had no choice but to take time off I discovered something interesting; the world actually didn't stop turning, my business opened and closed each day and guess what life went on!

It was during this period (a pretty low time for me) that I realised I needed to be more pro active if I wanted to be myself again and it lead me to work with a NLP practitioner. The experience affected me so profoundly that I trained to become one myself!

NLP helped me to gain a greater understanding and appreciation of myself and in turn I could adopt this attitude with others. Being able to communicate and appreciate yourself and the others around you makes for a healthier, happier world to live in!

My health is great; my business is going from strength to strength. I see my future and it looks marvellous!

Would I ever like to be that ill again? No, but thanks to it I have met some wonderful people and learned some amazing skills and it's going to keep happening because I know how not to get sick again!!"

Lorna Green
Edinburgh

Techniques mentioned
Mindset – belief, values

The futures bright!

"Since completing NLP Practitioner with Kirsty in Newcastle in March life journey has been amazing. I have attended many excellent personal development activities but none have produced the kick start I received through the combination of NLP Practitioner, followed a week later by a weekend retreat. During the retreat I reflected on my vision developed during the training and what I was going to do to bring it to life.

Together these activities have empowered me to make changes in my life I had only dreamed about up until now. I found the courage to resign my senior position within the blue chip company I had worked with for 19 years and have launched Karen Mason Associates.

Through my business activities I will fulfil my passion to work with private individuals and business leaders to ensure they get the best out of life and to inspire their teams. This will be achieved through personal development, coaching and consultancy utilising NLP techniques.

With the boundaries I set myself following NLP Practitioner life feels a lot more balanced, I have more time for my self development, quality time with my family and feel excited and committed to developing my business.

Thank you Kirsty for being part of my life transition.

Karen x"

Karen Mason
Preston

Techniques used:
Visualisation
Parts integration
Outcomes

Stuck in a moment

"The first is that the Fast Phobia Model that you used with me does appear to have effectively dealt with my claustrophobia. Although I have now been back in situations that previously would have brought on a panic attack I do not react in the same way as before. The worst I seem to feel is a sense of irritation but the urge to flee the situation, to get out, as quickly as possible has gone. I know I have a choice and I now choose not to be spooked! One of the things that helps is recalling the image of you singing, in your rather impressive fruity operatic mezzo voice, "Let me out, let me out, let me out" which has an effect on me like a chuckle-knuckle (though not as impressive as Kevin's!).

The other thing is in many ways much more personal and more profound, although I accept that others may not necessarily be able to see the significance. This is something that occurred during our week with you in March here in Newcastle during one of the exercises, which I think was placing a goal in the future.

One of the things that is important to me is mindfulness meditation, which I have practised on and off for some years. I find it very useful in my life generally and have of late been working on ways to integrate the meditation practice into my coaching work.

Earlier this year I found myself thinking about and feeling the need to develop and take my meditation practice to a higher level. To do so I felt that I needed to find a teacher or 'guru', my own Zen master. I had not made any progress on this by the time I came to do my NLP training so used this as one of the things I could work on for myself during the training.

The particular incident I have in mind happened (so far as I can recall - it turned out to be a very highly emotionally charged moment and although I retain it in startling clarity some of the context in which it occurred has faded somewhat) while doing the exercise of putting a goal into the future. What I did was choose the goal of finding that teacher and decided I wanted it to be accomplished by August of this year.

I had a very clear, sharp image of me sitting in my garden room, in dappled sunlight coming through the tomato plants I grow there, meditating with my teacher. What I had not expected, and what I had not intended, was that I found I could not actually see my teacher. Out of the field of my vision there was someone else, someone I could not see but who I could hear, and who I know with absolute certainty was my teacher.

What he told me was that I no longer needed him, that I already knew what I needed to know and what to do. He said it very simply and calmly but in a way that made him sound happy, not for himself but for me. My immediate feeling was one that I can only describe as being like grief. Here was someone that, although consciously I never actually knew him, I nevertheless felt a very deep affection and respect for, a profound connection. I felt as if I had just been parted from someone that I loved, although not entirely lost in spirit. (Just typing this now I feel the emotion welling within me again.) But I also felt honoured to be so loved in return, and trusted.

I then did not exactly forget about this unexpected development of or change in my goal but I did not exactly forget about it either and did not, consciously at least, do anything more definite about finding my teacher.

Later, in July, I was in Barcelona with Sally where she was attending the World Congress of Cognitive and Behavioural Therapists as her 'significant other'. Amusing myself by browsing among the book stands that always seem to go with these conferences I came across a few interesting books on mindfulness meditation itself and on some connections and uses of mindfulness in psychotherapeutic practice.

Back in the UK I tracked some of them down through Amazon (praise be the power of the discount!). Then one morning in August, reading one of these books on the train on the way into work I realised that this was what I had been looking for, that I knew what I needed and wanted to know. The book did not really tell me anything that I did not already know but it did help me realise what it is that I know and what I need and want to do. The sound of my unseen teacher's voice came back came back to me loud and clear. I would not say that it was a moment of enlightenment but it was nevertheless a deep and significant realisation - that the resources that I need are already there within me, that I just have to see that and use them.

Of more immediate practical importance what suddenly hit me was the idea for a book of my own on mindfulness meditation and coaching that I am now working on. Whether it finally sees the light of day remains to be seen but it is now a very real project that I will learn from and benefit from in any event regardless.

Time for me to insert another goal into my time line?"

Mark Robinson
Newcastle

Techniques used:
Fast Phobia Model
Logical levels of therapy
Setting achievable outcomes
Time Line Therapy™

The illusion of reality

"In fact what I have come to realise is this: as important as it is to hold a positive intention towards the people you're working with and have a best-case-scenario-outcome for them in your own mind, at the end of the day, people determine their own results. I know that this is emphasised throughout the NLP courses but it only really sank in with my own experience. As a practitioner you can only help someone find new ways of thinking and show them techniques that help them create more empowering choices for themselves. What they actually choose to do with that knowledge is strictly up to them. People have to want to be helped; they have to want to change their lives before anything can happen. It's up to them to want better for themselves. They have to be ready to effect change before anything can change. One can help by providing an environment conducive to that change and then just hope for the best. When clients are ready, all we do is facilitate the process.

My own struggle with NLP in the last year was with figuring out how something as simple as language and visualisation could be so powerful and effect so much change in anyone's life. I had to be 100% convinced in my own mind about how the process works so that I could channel that confidence in the process to persons with whom I interact.

This was my question and I encourage everyone to ask questions. Questions are important because they provide a frame or a context within which the answer can exist. The way I figure it, we're always surrounded by a field of all answers and asking the right question draws out the answer; it makes the answer perceivable to us when we "happen" upon it.

I think I was looking for an explanation of the link between language and reality. In the event that this might make sense to someone else out there, I will share what I found. If it doesn't make any sense and merely raises more questions in your own mind...all I can advise folk to do is to follow them until you find answers that feel right to you.

So here's the story.

A friend of mine who practices NLP among a lot of other things had taken down his website for a long time and recently posted it back up. When he did, a line in one of his opening WebPages read "Romance is an illusion." Somehow, reading that line formulated the answer to the question I had. Funny how the most apparently simple things can fire off your neurons and trigger intuitive learning's that help you fill in the blanks!

Anyhow, with my background and beliefs of how the Universe works, this is what I got. (The thing about my beliefs though, was that I almost had to forget them and rediscover them in order to realise their power!) So anyways, I found an answer to my question: how does the link between language and reality work?

All of life is an illusion anyway and romance is a part of life, just like you are and I am. So romance must be an illusion!

The Vedas call it "Maya"...often simply translated (and mistranslated) into "illusion."

Maya really means the manifestation of the One God as the multiplicity of forms in the material universe; the ignorance that draws a veil over the face of the One Reality so that all we see is diversity and Maya is the wisdom that ultimately leads us to pierce the veil and see the One beneath the many.

Romance is an illusion...life is an illusion.

If all we are is The Self, curving out from and back onto The Self, to rediscover The Self on this journey called life...then all of life really is an illusion! (From the Upanishads / Vedas.)

Romance is an illusion... Life is an illusion... Reality is an illusion!

Reality is an illusion.
Reality is a construction of Consciousness and thought.

We actively create reality through our perception of time, space, matter and energy.
We create whatever we observe and perceive with the power of our minds.

Our observations are measurements that transform the seamless infinity of everything into the boundaries and definitions of something.

Our measurements have the capacity to transform the infinite continuum of energy and consciousness that is everything into something specific ...an answer... a solution ... hope ... the perception of a moment where we are greater than our individual selves.

So, by measuring for something, even something intangible like meaning, we create it. We call it into being.

We measure reality into existence with the power of our words, with the power of our language.

All thoughts, even the ones unspoken exist in the form of language ... and what is language but sound energy?

The energy of unspoken thought represents the potential energy of sound and the energy of thoughts expressed represents the kinetic energy of sound.

The energy of sound has the power to inspire change in akash or ether (of the 5 elements of creation: earth, water, wind fire and akash (- Sanskrit, that which pervades everything; a conscious medium within which matter and energy can manifest. The Greeks call it "Ether" and the American Indians call it "Spirit.")

So, the energy of our thoughts creates our reality ... the one reality we choose out of an infinity of possibilities.

Reality is a creation of thought. Your reality is your creation. Your reality is created by your language.

There it was – the link between language and what you manifest in your life. Now that I understand it, I can make it work for me and use to help those who want to be helped.

So I mailed my friend all the things highlighted above. The next time I checked that line on my friend's website read "Romance might be an illusion."
We measured it into another definition, "Romance is the shakti (power / potential / strength) and beauty inherent in all of life." His website is down again...I don't know what that means".

Nisha Kissoon
Trinidad

Techniques used:
Mindset
Language and its power

I'll do it my way

"Well, I'm not quite sure where to start or what to say. My life has changed so dramatically in every way over the past 4 years that I could write a book about it.

Just four years ago I was miserable, depressed, lacked confidence and self esteem, viewed the world through blinkers, suffered from chronic fatigue and basically thought there was no hope for me. Somewhere deep inside me (so deep, in fact, I'm not sure I was aware of it consciously) I sensed that there was more to life - there had to be, otherwise what was the point? It was this feeling, deep inside me that got me where I am today – with a little help along the way.

I had a reasonably happy childhood up until I was 12, when my parents divorced after years of constant arguing. From that moment on I only had one goal in life and that was to leave home as soon as I could. I didn't focus on anything else; I had no other goals and probably not very much hope.

I became very depressed and spent most of my time sleeping, mainly to avoid my mum who was going through issues of her own at the time. It took 13 years before I was finally in a position where I could afford to leave home and buy a flat, so I did. It was around this time I met my boyfriend who moved into my new flat with me. The novelty of having my own place didn't last all that long – don't get me wrong, I was extremely grateful for what I had - but I hadn't resolved any of my underlying issues.

I eventually got engaged, moved into a really nice house, found myself a fantastic job and spent time with my family and friends, but I was still miserable and depressed most of the time and felt that life was something that had to be endured. I had everything our culture tends to promote and yet I still wasn't happy! I'd come to the end of the road so to speak. My fiancé told me I had to get counselling or some sort of help or he would leave me. Being afraid of asking people for help, fearing they would shun or ridicule me, I didn't get counselling. We eventually broke up - I'd reached rock bottom and there appeared to be no way out!

I decided the only option was to run away!!

I quit my job, sold my car and my house and booked a one way ticket to Russia (it took me a year to build up the courage to do it!!). Having said my goodbyes I boarded a plane one morning back in 2003 and didn't look back.

Having never travelled anywhere on my own and having a fear of approaching people and starting conversations I decided to throw myself in at the deep end. I figured if I could survive Russia, I could pretty much survive anything. I did survive - although the first few months were hell.

Here I was having the experience of a lifetime and I was miserable, but I was learning a lot about myself and gradually coming out of my depression. When there's no one around to take your anger out on, the anger dissipates fairly rapidly (that was my first huge lesson). I met lots of people (many of whom

I'm still friends with today), I saw amazing sights and I had more experiences than some people have in a lifetime. I was pushed out of my comfort zone on so many occasions. I'd been a fussy eater since I was two years old – I'll eat anything now. Travelling was better than any therapy I could have had!

While in New Zealand I met someone who became a very close friend. We both ended up in the same place following a random course of events. Neither of us should have been there but there was obviously a reason for it. This was my first taste of the universe conspiring to create events – destiny or coincidence?

Well, it was through meeting this person that I was introduced to NLP. When we met neither of us knew much about it all but that was all about to change through a chance meeting with an NLP Practitioner. While my friend had a very life changing conversation I was getting the first violin lesson I'd had in over 20 years (but that's another story). This had planted the seed in my friend's mind and on her return home she took a Practitioner course.

I returned home in 2005 for a brief stay before heading off again with my aforementioned friend. While travelling we did some Time Line Therapy™ and other NLP techniques which brought around some profound changes and planted the seed in me to become a practitioner.

While in Sydney I met the trainer my friend had trained with. After a few weeks of deliberating I booked on a course and on my return to the UK in spring 2006 I did my Practitioner training.

Having been through all this I was changed in ways I didn't realise was possible. My blinkers were gone and I had a different outlook on life, but there was still something holding me back, something deep inside that I couldn't articulate. I knew it was there but had no idea what it was or how I could get rid of it.

I went on to do the Time Line Therapy™ course which I thought might help but it didn't – after this I plucked up the courage to ask my trainer if we could have a one-to-one session, I still wasn't comfortable with asking people for help at this point, but I knew I needed to do it!

I had a session with her and it helped to alleviate a lot of issues that were holding me back. Now I can go up to complete strangers and ask them for help, which may not seem huge, but to me it was life changing. It's such a profound change externally but internally it feels incredibly subtle. You know something's changed – but you can't quite put your finger on what it is! It's almost like you have to play with life after a TLT session to see how it's changed you.

Even 8 months on from the session I'm still surprising myself by doing things I previously thought I'd never do without even thinking about what I'm doing.

Anyway, after the Time Line Therapy™ session I was on a roll but I still felt I had some way to go. I wasn't confident practising my TLT skills with people. I didn't have belief in my own skills - I was scared it wouldn't work, worried that I would say the wrong thing and a multitude of other negative thoughts running through my head. For much of the same reasons I felt I couldn't go on to do the Master Practitioner course. There were also a few other things in my life holding me back.

This all changed when I decided to go on a weeklong firewalking initiation course. During the course of this week I was pushed outside my comfort zone on so many occasions, but the results were more than worth it. At the end of the week we had a chance to share with the group what we'd been through and this is pretty much what I said: "Before coming on Initiation I felt that my life just didn't make any sense. Now it all makes perfect sense!" Again this was a hugely profound change deep inside me which I cannot put into words, I've no idea how or why life makes sense now, I just know that it does.

Nowadays I have goals, so many of them in fact I'm having to prioritise them. I'm learning to play the fiddle, studying nutrition, helping people to change their lives using TLT, fire walking whenever I get the chance, manifesting the means to pay for my Master Practitioner course and learning Spanish (in preparation for a trip to S. Amercia) amongst other things. I'm discovering new things every day that I want to experience. I'm currently discovering the magic of manifestation – it really does work – and I'm having so much fun playing with it! I'M HAPPY!

Just four years ago I could never have realised in my wildest dreams that I'd be where I am now and what is possible. Now I know that anything and everything is possible! I've now reached a turning point on my path and I'm ready to move forward to wherever my life takes me. Knowing what is possible, I want to do all I can to help others discover the magic of life and realise that their hopes and dreams can be real. I'm going to continue exploring and learning new ways of doing this - Master Prac here I come....

Hilary Thain
Glasgow

Techniques mentioned:
Time Line Therapy™

That was easy!

"I started with Excelr8 back in January 2008 and my life has transformed dramatically............

I have known Kirst for a few years and following the success of the business in 2006 she realised that she needed a wee assistant, enter Moi! Now, I had always been fascinated in the world that Kirsty operated so I assumed (and boy was I right) that embarking on a career with her would be somewhat interesting, exciting, educational and different to anything I have ever done before.
Where do I sign?

Within the first week I had floated above my Time Line squashing limiting beliefs and negative emotions, set goals and had been introduced to the Tad and watched the Secret!
Wow! Trying to explain this to mum was a task in itself!!

One particular limiting decision we worked on was my fear of driving......I am originally from a small Scottish Island with one road the whole way round so when moving up to the big smoke and faced with round-a bouts, traffic lights and more than a few cars on the road I was naturally put off. That day when I was 17 and drove on the mainland for the first time – I decided would be my last time.
Enter Kirsty 10 years later.....
Now I had successfully nurtured my limiting decision for years and managed to get around it but that that first day I started with Kirsty she had me floating above my Time Line and dealing

with it. What came out was truly fascinating – so here I am back in my past 3 years old and I am crying in the back seat of a blue Volvo with sea to the right of me and a man shouting at my mum. Mum was on the mainland and had gone into the back of a man's car and from that day on I decided that driving on the mainland meant crashes and people shouting at you!! Genius!! Well I learnt from that and all other experiences on my Time Line and I now drive on the mainland in fact I am so confident I am actually thinking of driving a taxi in my spare time!!!!

I was the queen of procrastination and previously I thought joining a gym for a year would automatically transform me to a toned size 8, I have lived this motto for many years spending a fortune on an unused gym membership while my trendy outfit (labels and all) was gathering dust at the back of my wardrobe. I needed to change but never found the time, that was until my practitioner training in February 2008.........My main objective was find the time and hit the gym and since then I have not looked back.

I now attend 5 classes a week and am not a size 8 (YET!) but am a lot closer than I ever dreamed. One of my goals I set was to compete in the Great Scottish Run in September (which I had been saying for years but never bothered).

I put a lot of deep HA breaths into that goal and come September I ran the 10k in 57 minutes and raised over £500 for charity...........this stuff works!!!

I have also created a vision board and already removed a few things as they have been achieved; I have been to see Madonna; got free tickets to T in the Park; received free VIP tickets to the Red Hot Chilli Peppers; GHD straighteners the list goes on and on - ....this stuff works!!! "

Ailie Duncan
Isle of Arran

Techniques mentioned:
Time Line Therapy™
Outcomes – setting achievable outcomes
Chaining anchors
Law of Attraction

Fore!

"Recently I attended an interview for a job as a trainer at an exclusive Business Training Academy. Prior to the interview, although I felt well prepared, I nevertheless anchored two states, calm and confident. The interview went incredibly well and the future looks promising.

The process of Anchoring has become a well worn habit and always results in the performance I visualised. This is particularly important in my profession as a Management trainer, English teacher and Golf coach.

For those who suffer from perfectly natural pre- performance nerves, this simple process can put you in the state of mind you want to enable you to realise your true potential.

The other process of visualising the results you want e.g. prior to hitting a golf ball or going into a meeting is also extremely powerful. My fellow golfers have commented on how cool I am under pressure, unaware of the NLP process of Anchoring.

When I am coaching very good golfers who suffer from tension, I recommend this technique. It really is a performance enhancer and so easy to do.

I have passed on this very simple skill to my daughter who is also a teacher, my mother when she is feeling sad, and my mother in law to give her confidence. Even my wife who is an opera singer is coming around to the Anchoring process prior to a big performance".

Bill Cole
Germany

Techniques mentioned:
Anchoring
Visualisation

Metaphorically speaking

"My life changing events happened on my NLP Practitioners course in August this year, the first was on the day we learnt about Metaphors.

We were working in groups of three and I was the client, my problem being discussed was my fear of doing presentations, I also had to disclose my hobbies and interests, after which I was asked to leave the room whilst my colleges decided on a suitable Metaphor, when I was then invited back to hear it.

The practitioner then proceeded to tell me a lovely story about walking in the Lake District, however, during the story I began to feel very emotional which progressed to me being in tears, but couldn't understand why and for some reason I felt 'lighter'.

That afternoon I stood in front of the group and delivered the three Metaphors we had been set for homework without palpations or sweaty palms or any abdominal problems that usually accompany even the hint of having to deliver a presentation, it was magic!

On my way home in the car I felt a new found confidence, but every time I tried to rationalise what caused the tears it just evoked the same state, not a good idea whilst driving. So now I have stopped trying to work out why it worked, instead I rejoice in the fact it did.

My second event was 'The Big One' it happened when we were learning about Time Line Therapy™, for this we worked in pairs, but we were over seen by our trainer who asked me what problem I wanted to work on, so after numerous "so how is that a problem?" later it was established my problem was I didn't think I was normal which on voicing this made me cry.

Kirsty then took charge of the therapy and floated me back along my time line to the first event, which interestingly was 8 months in the womb (mind blowing!). When I reached the event I experienced the most overwhelming feeling of emotions, which I can't begin to express in words, but thankfully I didn't have to endure long as Kirsty floated me up high above the event so my distress was manageable and very quickly no more.

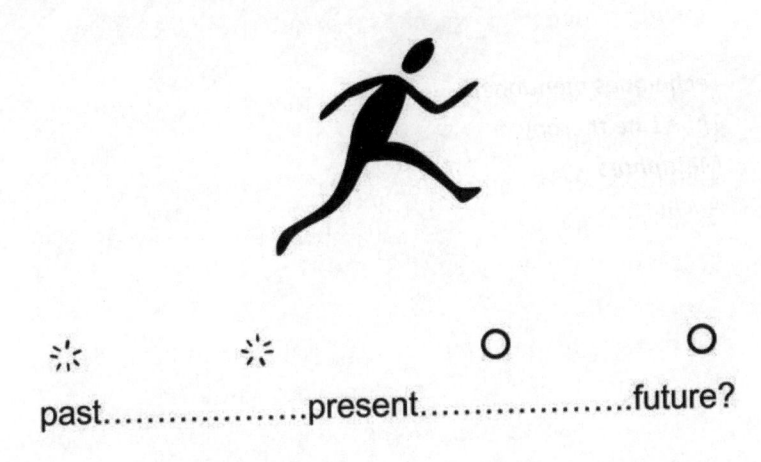

past...............present...............future?

As I then floated back along my time line to present day it was like sorting through a page a day diary for the whole of my 51 years but the feeling of not been normal was no longer present,

That night I went home a different person looking at the world through fresh eyes and I felt amazing, when I went into the course next morning I was asked, had I had a face peel, as I looked younger.

At the end of the course Kirsty asked me where the Ann had gone who had started the course, because I had changed so much in a week!

I don't know or care where the old Ann went I love this new one so much that I too want to be a trainer to teach people this fantastic therapy that really does change lives!"

Ann Douglas
Leeds

Techniques mentioned:
Time Line therapy™
Metaphors
Anchors

Lights, camera, action!

"Just a final couple of notes about stuff happening at this end.

I told you my 16 year old son is a great believer in all of the NLP stuff and regularly re-watches the Secret. He applies the law of attraction to almost everything from hoping someone will phone him to take his shift at the local restaurant where he works to forming relationships with influencers who can help him with his career moves, all of which are working (small things but nevertheless true).

Last week he performed in London's West End at "Her Majesty's Theatre" in a variety show (something he wished for and applied via the Internet). Since then so many people have noticed him and he has featured in the press locally and back in his home city of Newcastle. He has now set his sights on a place as an extra on Coronation Street or one of the other soaps and is confident that the letters he is writing now will bear fruit (I will let you know on this one).

As for me, I think I remarked in a recent e-mail that I was worried about not being confident about the techniques and strategies I applied when asked to help on a phobia of flying. Apparently I must have been on the right lines because the person concerned has just returned from France having had a great flight!

Following the Hypnotherapy course I have downloaded some of the scripts from one of the Internet sites Kirsty recommended in the back of her workbook. I have re-written the Dave Elman induction in my format **(yes with highlighted bits!)** and I am using some of those scripts with my wife and son to address various concerns they have with self-confidence) I will be using other techniques alongside but I really want to become proficient at the relaxation exercises. So I will let you know how this works in due course"

Kevin Charlton
Cheshire

Techniques mentioned
Mindset – Law of Attraction, focus
Techniques – Fast phobia model, hypnotherapy

Presenting Magically

"There are many trains of thought that surround the success of NLP. Some people are skeptical about its effects, other people tend to buy into the concept of what it can achieve for them whole-heartedly and immerse themselves into it with such enthusiasm that it feeds through all facets of their lifestyle.

Whichever one you are, there is no doubt that NLP will play an important place in your lifestyle be it in a business or personal setting.

As for me....my interest in NLP started off as being purely for business. As I work in the health and safety profession, I was keen to find different ways to engage with people to ensure that the safety message was heard. Unfortunately it is often the case that people are resistant to these messages for any number of distorting factors (i.e. previous experiences, upbringing, etc, etc).

The NLP course simply provided me with an extra set of tools that I am able to use to find different and exciting ways to engage with people. I explain it to people by saying that it provides me with "an edge" when dealing with situations as I feel that I have more options and flexibility to cope with any of the twists and turns that could occur.

My most memorable experience of using NLP since completing the course was during a presentation that I was delivering to a group of 70 new starters with the company. As per usual, the butterflies were whirling around my stomach and I was frantically trying to remember my lines for fear of looking like I did not know what I was talking about. Whilst I was sat there waiting...worrying, I started to search my memory banks for a technique that I could use to prepare for the presentation. The most fundamental thing that I learnt on the NLP course is that you are 100% in control of your state at all times and once you understand this, it can benefit you in every aspect of your life.

So whilst I was waiting...worrying....I started to visualise myself stood up in front of the group, confident, loud and professional. I imagined myself being able to connect with every member of the group by using just my voice and body language and I visualised the group understanding and accepting the messages that I was there to put across.

Then it was time....I stood up, walked into the room and delivered the best presentation of my life, it was slick, witty and professional. I could even tell that the group was with me every step of the way as their body language was different also...attentive, interested and thirsty for more. It was then that the true benefits of what I had learned on the NLP course hit me and for the first time I truly felt like I had "the edge".

So whatever you are looking to get out of NLP, be it in a business setting or a personal interest I know that you will find it a rewarding and beneficial skill to keep in your toolkit for life."

Steve Broom
Southampton

Techniques mentioned:
Visualisation
Rapport
Anchoring
Mindset – state control

TLTing at Windmills

"One evening recently, sitting with my wife we got round to talking about childhood times and how they felt. Both she and I had been lucky in having great childhoods and as we reminisced about our separate upbringings the chat became more towards recent times. Anyway as we chatted I suggested I would like to use some Time Line Therapy™ to practice my skills and to see if there was any unwanted emotion she would like to be rid of.

With a bit of Milton language to help she relaxed and raised a feeling that she had about one of her parents that she got from time to time and was not sure where it came from. A bit more 'trance' inducing chat and then we moved into a Time Line Therapy™ session. Having established her timeline we moved above it to the point where this particular emotion was first felt. It seems that it was when she was a few months old. As we moved back along the timeline we came to a place where she could no longer feel that emotion.

Talking her through the process we eventually came back into the room - and now she no longer has feels that niggling emotion when recalling her childhood or when she thinks of that parent today! "

David Kelly
Bexhill-on-sea
Techniques used:
Time Line Therapy™

Spider schmider!

"I have used my learning's from the NLP practitioner's course many times to improve the lives of service personnel within the Royal Air Force.

One in particular was the padre, who had a phobia of spiders. When he found out I had done the course, and once I explained what NLP was, he was more than happy to give it a try. Using the fast phobia technique and Time Line Therapy™, I managed to help him turn his fear into a positive. After the session I showed him a picture of a spider, which he took and laughed at!

In the past even a picture would have sent him screaming from the room like a banshee!! That night we all met up for an important Dinning In event (dinner party), and out of the blue a spider crawls across the table in front of the padre.

Everyone looks at him expecting a right old show of screams and wailing, but it never came. He just picked it up gently and placed it on the floor, to the shock and disappointment of a few lookers on. All thanks to the wonderment of NLP...."

Simon Almond
Leucars

Techniques used:
Time Line Therapy™
Fast Phobia Model

Still no collywobbles!

"For as long as I can remember I have always had a hatred of speaking in public. I remember even in primary school just standing in class crying because I could not speak. I always dreaded the Friday session in secondary school when one of the teachers used to get us to read from the set novel. I just wished that someone would mention the war and then the teacher would be off on a tangent, on his war experiences, and a sigh of relief from me.

I had done a few small bits of training over the years, but usually on topics that I knew like the back of my hand, the audience were usually my juniors. Even then I always had the collywobbles until it was over.

A few years ago I was a participant in a seminar on immunisation. Following this one of the facilitators asked me to be one of the facilitators on the course in 2007. For some reason I said yes............what was I thinking about, this is not an hour or even a day's training session, it's a 6 days seminar..........So even way back in December 2006 just thinking about it ....yep you've guessed it I got the collywobbles.

In Feb 2007 I attended the practitioner course and SWISH the collywobbles have gone.

The big (for me) seminar starts in just over 2 week's time, There will be about 15 participants in the group of my peers, including 2 of my previous bosses. I just heard this afternoon that one of my co presenters who is working in Myanmar (Burma) will not be able to attend the seminar, because of the problems there. I heard myself volunteering to take over one of his sessions, which is the foundation of the whole seminar............and still no Collywobbles....."

Frances Devlin
London, Ireland and the rest of the world

Techniques used:
Submodalities – swish pattern

I'm in the money!

"Wait until you hear my news! After I watched the Secret, I think I told you that I wrote some stuff down, one of which was that I was happy and grateful to have £2000 (which I had in my mind to pay off the last of my travel debts).

Well, this week I got news that I was getting an unexpected bonus at work (of £1000) and yesterday I received a cheque from the Inland Revenue for over £2000 in overpaid tax whilst I was out the country!
Waaaa!!!

I honestly couldn't believe it! So there you go, another one for your book! I've now officially paid off all my travel debts! Hurrah!
Have a great one"

Susan Perry
Glasgow

Techniques used:
Law of attraction
Mindset: Focus on outcomes

Any dream will do!

"NLP has made me so positive about life; energetic and excited! The anchoring is working like magic for me; yes sometimes it's annoying for the people around because they are so used to not seeing someone so positive, energetic and enthusiastic with my new energy!

I am surprised to see people who never spoke to me come up to me and say hello, not just hello but they seem to be excited to see me and meet me!

Maybe their unconscious can feel the energy which I am carrying. Wow- what a change in people's attitude towards me...
Another thing...

Kirsty did Time Line Therapy™ with us and she knows what happened afterwards! We were supposed to help each other remove our conflicts by parts integration but the Time Line Therapy ™worked wonders for me and I didn't have any conflicts anymore.

I had my first goal of buying a house by 29th October 2007.

And I am proud to say that, I have bought my house and will be shifting in my house by 11th October 2007.

All thanks to Kirsty and NLP
Thanks a lot
I am enjoying every day and everyone in my life

I know I can achieve the impossible, I know I can :)"

Rahul Patil
Mumbai

Techniques used:
Anchoring
Time Line Therapy™
Outcomes

Part 2

How to do the techniques

"Yesterday is history. Tomorrow is a mystery. And today? Today is a gift. That's why we call it the present".
Babatunde Olatunji

This part of the book will talk you through some of the techniques from NLP and the mindset. The techniques mentioned here are in no way the absolute all of NLP, if anything, they are only the tip of an iceberg!

You can see what the students and clients achieved. The exercises are for you to experience what it is possible for yourself. With all of the exercises that create change, check with yourself that it is OK to make that change.

A lot of the exercises are good to do with a partner, so grab someone and ask them to help you in your NLP journey of discovery!

It's an Inside Job

We need to start being consciously aware of all of these elements. Here we are going to look at our filters and the mindset frames that we talk about within NLP.

Unconscious Filters

NLP looks at your filters as lenses on reality; they determine what information we receive from the world. They are a sieve, a way of us sorting the world. They determine what we see.

"You don't believe what you see, you see what you believe"

Values

Values are relatively unconscious filters. They determine what we think is good or bad, and what we will or won't do. They are not necessarily what we like or do not like; they are what we deem to be important.

Values have 2 purposes - creating who we are and what we do – they determine how we spend our time (you won't do something that is not important to you) and they determine our evaluations – whether what we did was right or wrong/good or bad.

They determine how we feel about self or others. They are more conscious then meta-programs and more unconscious than beliefs. Values create our motivation; what do we need to do with our time. Pretty important then huh?

Working with values gives you more leverage. If we take out the value we change the beliefs.

Beliefs

Invariably there can be many beliefs attached to a value as values are the controlling element of the beliefs. Beliefs are those convictions which we trust as being true. They generally tend to empower or dis-empower us, more so than values. They can determine what we can and cannot do. They provide a rules structure as to how we relate to certain events. Your beliefs can help you to wealth, health and happiness or they can keep you poor, unwell and downright miserable.

Metaprogrammes

These are deeply unconscious filters that define personal and work behaviour. Understanding these will help you determine how you live your life.

Memories

Everything that has ever happened to us is held within our unconscious minds. Everything! They first started to discover this with the Penfield Study in 1957. Memories can guide your present life even though you don't do it consciously. I have a client who is vehement about marriage – infact, finds weddings annoying and irritating as "people just don't know what they are agreeing to, they don't know the meaning of it". His father had an affair when he was younger which led to his parents' divorce.

Again this is an example of generalisation whereby he has categorised all weddings and couples in the same light as his parents. His negative memories of marriage are holding him back from seeing options, and, not opening him up to a relationship whereby he can get married and live happily ever after.

If there are a lot of negative emotions attached to our memories, then we can be filtering out/ignoring what else is available to us in a positive nature. By releasing negative emotions on memories, you can change how someone views the world.

Attitude

Our attitude is our filtration system to our life. We can change our attitude alone, without any circumstances changing in our external world, and we can change our life. To continue the computer analogy, it is our firewall; it determines what gets through and what doesn't. You know yourself that when you have a "can do anything "attitude then you are able to tackle events and challenges.

Cause and Effect

In NLP, one of the key frames we talk about is Cause and effect. What does this mean? Well, there are some people in life that are on the effect side of the equation. They will recount excuse upon excuse as reasons to tell you why they haven't achieved what they wanted to achieve in their life. Some people are happy to have excuses, and limiting beliefs. They know all the reasons for failure and have what they believe to be airtight alibis, reasons to explain away their own lack of achievement.

"If only I had money"
"If I only hadn't got married earlier"
"Marketing never provide us with the right materials to sell"
"I never had the right equipment to do the job"

Imagine this now, close your eyes and imagine, you get to your rocking chair in the nursing home and you are sitting talking to your family.

What do you see, what do you hear and what do you feel?

Are you saying "Oh, I wish I had done this, I wish I had completed this job however I couldn't do that because someone else had gone there before me? I couldn't do this in my life because of my ex wife or ex husband" OR are you saying "wow - how good was that?"

You can make a choice now to be on the cause side of the equation and produce results and be the cause of what happens to you in your life. Or you can continue with excuses and live life as a victim.

There are many people in life that are happy to survive rather than thrive... they are happy to be "not sick". What would happen if you decided, now, to be choosing and causing what happens in your life?

There's a wonderful man who has inspired me, Miles Hilton Barber who says "the only limits in life are those you accept yourself". He decided not to allow the value of his life to decrease when he turned blind in his twenties and has achieved more than most in the preceding years – he's wing walked, he's skydived about 40 times and has just come back from circumnavigating the globe in a micro light aircraft! (His call sign is batman as he is as blind as a bat!).

We can choose whether to be at the effect of what happens in our lives or we can choose, now to be in control. We are driving the bus! Grab the steering wheel!

I was handed a quote today from a student and I think it sums up Cause and effect – in a way!

"Life should NOT be a journey to the grave with the intention of arriving safely in an attractive and well- preserved body, but rather to skid in sideways, champagne in one hand, strawberries in the other, body thoroughly used up, totally worn out and screaming 'WOO HOO – what a ride!"

Comfort zone

Are you operating at your optimum or are you quite happy to doddle along on the treadmill of life? Do you continuously test yourself and see what you are capable of? How about you decide to step out your comfort zone in an area of your life now?

What are you focusing on?

We have within our minds something called our **Reticular Activating System.** Ensure you are focusing on what you want; the search engine can be activated and will search through all the pages until it find a perfect match i.e. exactly what you don't want or what you do want.

Our RAS is like a homing device; it goes out and finds items and resources that are important to you and your outcomes. Have you ever bought a new item of clothing and know and feel happy that it was 'slightly obscure' not everyone had one? Well, what happens when you buy it? Yes, you seem to see them *everywhere*. No matter where we look, there's someone else wearing it!

Our RAS can also be affected by our beliefs. If we believe that we are just unlucky, nothing good *ever* happens to us, then we activate our RAS to make sure that that happens! Even if a good situation or circumstance came and slapped us on the face then we would still be closed to the possibility.

The L word

Even though our communication shows that 7% is through our language it is very important. Invariably we do not think about what comes out of our mouth, it's unconscious.

We need to be able to use this unconscious communication consciously.

Language is also one of our filters and therefore will change what we view in the world. After I learnt about NLP, it never ceases to amaze me how we do actually communicate with each other - essentially, we all talk different languages!

On top of being predominantly visual, auditory or kinaesthetic, some of us like detail, some big picture. We make assumptions in people's speech about what they say; there are many deletions, distortions and generalisations that take place sentence by sentence. We can use our language to eloquently tell a story and help loosen the client's model of the world.

Here we are going to talk about the precision of language (until we get to Milton Model which is ambiguously precise!) and how to use our words consciously.

It's not a negative thing!

Our brains cannot process a negative. No easy way to write that! Before we start this, just close your eyes and clear your mind, remove all thoughts from your mind and do not think about your bedroom, do not think about anything in your bedroom, no thought of your bedroom to be in your mind, now! I know, you are thinking of your bedroom! It's a two step process that happens in our minds. In order to not think of your bedroom, you have to think about your bedroom first and then wipe the image away.

So, think about the language we use on a daily basis. The first word we learn as a child? "No!" "Don't do that!"

"I do not want an argument with you"
= *"I want to argue with you"*
"I don't want to argue about your appraisal"
="I want to argue about your appraisal"
"Remember not to forget your keys! Don't forget your keys!"
="Forget your keys"

We need to learn to rephrase our language in the positive. Go on, give it a go!

I would *try* that *but*

How often do we use the words try or but? Both very important words; do we use them consciously?

Sttrreettccch

Find a pen or a pencil now. I want you to put it down next to you and really *try* and pick it up. Now I mean really *try* now. Did you pick it up? If you did, then you didn't try! If you picked up the pen then you did the process, trying means that you didn't. Trying implies not doing. When we hear peoples say "Well, I'll try the exercise", "I'm really going to try and go to the gym today" it invariably means that they won't actually be doing it!

So, avoid trying, do!

The word "but" is very important when you are giving feedback. It is of paramount importance when giving feedback to avoid the word "but".

E.g. "Your presentation was great, you covered off all the points required but your rapport with the group was poor"

The word "but" seems to negate everything that preceded it. It's as if you didn't say anything about it being a good presentation.

"Your presentation was great, you covered off all the points required and your rapport with the group wasn't as good as it usually is, overall a great, visual and informative presentation".

So, replace *but* with *and*. Makes a difference doesn't it?

How or why?

Again, just one word however it makes an impact. We tend to avoid the word why when questioning problems as it can be confrontational at times and can also limit the choices. Instead, we ask "how?"

"How is that a problem?" will give you much more information than "why is that a problem?"

Once upon a time...

Everyone loves a good story don't they? Metaphors are used daily, we live on stories. When we meet up with friends and family we relay stories, when we go to the cinema we watch stories, when we turn on the news; its news stories!

Daily phrases are metaphors;

"Quiet as a mouse" "He's such a wet blanket" "Clear as mud"

These phrases are generally accepted and known.

We use metaphors in NLP in different ways. We use them successfully in presentations as multiple embedded metaphors and in therapy and coaching with clients.

Our unconscious minds are symbolic and a metaphor works well to talk to the unconscious mind with solutions and resources. It's good to be able to use the story to connect with the unconscious mind, even if the conscious mind is frantically trying to work out what the point of the story is, your unconscious picks up the meanings. This is a powerful tool and bypasses the critical faculty that separates the conscious from the unconscious.

A story can be less direct, less personal (to the conscious mind!) and can displace resistance. Truth wrapped up in a story is "kinder".

Metaphors with clients

Ann Douglas (page 110) talked about the power of the story that her fellow students told her. She had no idea why she was getting this strong powerful emotion from the story, she accepted it and knows that it worked!

"Telling stories" with clients is a great technique to allow the client to make sense of what is happening and give them guidance, give them the plot of the story. In modelling Milton Erikson, the great hypnotherapist, Bandler and Grinder recognised his use of metaphors with his clients; some thought he was a 'rambler' however each of his stories had meaning and clarity for the client.

Children absorb stories and this can be a tool to enable them for change, to solve a problem, to address a challenge, with a story about their favourite super hero. Knowing what Bob the Builder or Spiderman would do in such a situation can assist the children in their circumstances.

If you can tell a story with vision, you can reframe and organise people's thoughts and ultimately change their behaviours.

STTTTRRreettCHH

Is there someone you know that has a particular challenge at the moment? Do you? Think of a story that aids the solution to that challenge. What are the person's interests and hobbies? Could you design a story for the person that aids them?

Presentations with metaphors

Think of all the great speakers of our time, they are able to weave stories and ideas and create a vision and a following. I use metaphors within trainings all the time, for different reasons. Some bring the theory to life, relaying a story of a client or business can assist the group in understanding the value and consequences of what the techniques can accomplish.

I start the days of training with multiple embedded metaphors (or nested loops) which create certain states and can be used to induce a light trance. A light trance is a good state to be in for learning, when you are in trance you are more in touch with your unconscious mind.

Multiple embedded metaphors can create curiosity and wondering as you do not finish the metaphors completely at the star of the day. You start one story but you don't complete it and then that leads you onto another story which you don't complete and then the next which you don't complete and then you can just begin the training.

The "audience" will be wondering if you are ever going to finish the stories and may look at you as if you have lost your marbles too! The embedded metaphors tell the listeners - you don't have it all yet! You only close the loops much later by finishing off each of the stories in reverse order.

Look at the example below:

"I used to be a runner, infact I came from a running family. My mum and dad ran marathons and my brother was a great hurdler and sprinter. I remember there was one time when we were practising our starts and my coach said something very odd to me. He said.....
When we travelled, we were lucky enough to go whale watching in a beautiful place called Kaikoura. It was a place caught in time with; everything was slow motion and peaceful. The morning of whale watching was still and quiet and the boat bounded over the waves like a bouncy ball. We stopped and looked out and saw a huge shape on the water. It was, essentially a huge blob, a mass. Nothing exciting and certainly not the national geographic picture of a whale that I was looking for. Then all of a sudden...
And I knew as soon as I stood on the bridge that I felt supremely calm about doing the bungee jump. The people there were great, the atmosphere electric and the view breathtaking. My number was called and I moved forward to where the put on all the bindings and straps. Strapped up safely I shuffled forward towards the edge, where my calmness slipped out of me through my trainers and down into the water below. Actually I was fine on the bridge, great view, I'll stay here. I knew I had to go there, however I was good on the bridge...

Content – *"well today we are going to talk about the use of language and its importance"* So here is where you do your presentation with the loops opened and without conclusions. At the end of the presentation you the close the loops.

"I've never wanted to jump off a bridge, I don't need to now! And then I jumped, and boy did I scream. I bounced on the rope and was then collected by the boat. Iain came towards me and asked me how it was "Can I do it again?" was my reply.

And then suddenly out of the water came this beautiful tail and you could see the beauty of the creature, the water spouted from the hole and the tail fanned out set on a background of snow-capped mountains. And then, it was gone.

He said, "Don't listen for the gun". It struck me as fairly odd to not listen for the gun because surely I had to, that would be what the rest of the runners would be doing! In the next race, I got to my blocks and had my coaches voice going round and round in my head "Don't listen for the gun, don't listen for the gun". On your marks! And I was into my stride at fifty metres and over the line before everyone else before I realised I hadn't heard the gun"

SSTTTrrettch

Gather together 3 metaphors/stories. Think of the meanings behind the stories, what insights, resources and thoughts could be triggered by the listener? In order to make use of these in a presentation you want to think about where to "stop them".

You will start to tell one of your stories and about 80-90% of the way through you break off so there is no conclusion. You then immediately lead into another story. You leave all three stories incomplete.

What specifically do you mean?

The Meta model is a model of language devised by Richard Bandler and John Grinder as a means of identifying problematic patterns in people's speech. Some of our verbal communication can be subject to considerable ambiguity and this can create limitation and a decrease in communication. It provides a set of questions for each category which can be used to specify and clarify and can transform potential limitations.

Distortions

"I know you will love this"
"I know she doesn't like me"
"You were good"

Distortion is where you change the meaning of the experience against your own reality; people sometimes don't realise that the distortion doesn't necessarily represent the truth. Mind reading is a great example of distortion; you can never know what someone else is thinking, we can make value judgements with mind reading.

Meta Model patterns	Examples of the patterns	Questions to help you gather more info
Mind reads	You're going to love this. You don't like me	How do you know that? How do you know I don't like you?
Lost performatives	It's bad to inconsistent. Its evil to be late	According to whom?
Complex equivalence	She's always shouting at me, she doesn't like me. With a name like that she must be popular	How does her shouting mean.. How does that name make her popular?
Cause and effect	You make me sad. I made her feel awful	How does what I'm doing cause you to choose to feel sad? How exactly did you do that?
Presuppositions	If she knew how much I suffered, she wouldn't do that	How do you choose to suffer? How do you know she doesn't know?

Generalisations

"It's always the same"
"I ought to call him"
"We never ever go out anymore!"

Generalisation is a skill and it can also limit us. If you have had a certain bad experience then we may think that it will happen time and time again. It can be quite a rigid and black and white style of thinking.

Meta Model patterns	Example of the patterns	Questions to help you gather more info
Universal Quantifiers	He never thinks about what I would like to do. She never listens to me	Never, ever? What would happen if she did?
Modal operators of necessity	I have to take care of her, we should, we ought to	What would happen if we didn't?
Modal operators of possibility	I can't do it. It's not possible	What prevents you?

Deletions

"Just do it"
"I don't know"
"I am uncomfortable"

Deletion delivers a valuable screening mechanism to prevent sensory overload from all the information we are inundated with. It can also restrict and limit our thinking and understanding.

Do you know someone who refuses to hear the compliments; only the criticisms?

Meta model patterns	Examples of the patterns	Questions to help you gather more info
Nominalisations	There is no communication here. Change is easy.	Who's not communicating what to whom? Changing what is easy?
Unspecified Verbs	He rejected me. She annoyed me.	How specifically?
Simple deletions	I've been out. I'm angry.	Where specifically have you been? What specifically are you angry about?

Lack of referential index	They never listen to me.	Who specifically doesn't listen to you?
Comparisons	She's a much better person. It's easier this way	Better at what than whom? Compared to what?

The Meta Model is great for clarifying the other persons meaning, gathering more information, discovering limitations (in self and others) and opening up more choices.

StttRRETCH!

To use the Meta model, listen to the words and start to spot the patterns in people's language. Intervene with the right question to open up choices and gather information.

And remember, rapport is of ultimate importance. If you are asking questions that may be unravelling someone's current model of the world then rapport is essential in order to 'soften' the questions.

Milton Model

Unlike the Meta model which is a series of questions that get specific details and increase choices, the Milton Model is decidedly vague. The Milton model language patterns are general and suggestive.

They are a series of language patterns that Milton Eriksson used with his patients. With the Milton model, people go into an altered state of consciousness whereby their conscious mind is distracted and the unconscious is ready and willing to listen to the therapist! The language used allows the client to work unconsciously in gaining new resources and insights.

The Meta model brings the resources into the conscious awareness and is specific whereas the Milton Model leads the client to do a trans-derivational search to access the resources.

Chunking!!

I used to work with someone who was explicitly detailed and meetings would last for an age when they were chairing. I'm happy with big picture and like to know the overall picture before moving forward into detail, when necessary!

People are comfortable with a certain level of detail. Some people are globally minded in that they want big picture/top line. Others are focussed solely on detail and need to know all the angles. Some will start a conversation and digress onto another story and then create tangents.

Think of people you work with, the Boss/CEO/Director of the company is paid the money to look at the big picture whereby all the different departments are focused on the detail of their specific roles.

The Milton model is a style of communication that moves upwards and focuses ideas at a highly general level; the Meta Model has a downward direction concentrating on very specific details.

Often when we use metaphors we are moving across sideways – chunking laterally – using the same level of detail and assisting people to access new resources and make new connections.

We need to be flexible enough to move up and down and across in order to be able to communicate with people on different levels.

Have you ever been in meetings about meetings? The end of the meeting is to organise the next meeting in order to talk about what you have just talked about in this meeting? Well, that's where chunking up is invaluable! Ask yourself, "What is the purpose of this? What is the intention of this?"

If you are requiring someone to focus on the detail you can ask, "what specifically? What are specific examples of this? Chunking laterally allows us to look at other examples and create new connections.

SSSTTTRREEETTCH

It's time to work on your chunking muscles! Grab someone else and see where your comfort zone is.

Do you like detail or big picture?

So, one of you has to come up with a word, any word. Then the other one has to either get you to chunk up, chunk down or chunk laterally.

To chunk up – ask the question "For what purpose? Or what is the intention of this/that?"

To chunk down – ask the question "What are specific examples of these? What specifically?"

To chunk laterally – ask the question "What are other examples of these?

Keep doing this and change the questions you are using. You will soon find out where your comfort zone is. Play around with the other areas to expand your comfort zone.

What are you saying to yourself?

There are times when we talk to ourselves – go on admit it! And we need to be very clear about what we are saying to ourselves.

I had a client who told me that she never had enough time. In fact, during our 10 minute conversation she said she "never had enough time, I've got too much to do" – 25 times! So, over a 10 hour period that could be 1500 times! Over a 5 day working week 7500 times!

Now that's a time stealer in itself!

So, to promote self awareness, I asked her to mark down any time she said she had an issue with time.

She now goes to the gym 4 times a week, has organised her entire wedding (previously too stressed to even think about it) and has lost 1 and a half stone.

She admits that when she got to marking down the 15th time of complaining about time she'd had enough and decided to create time – she is now renowned for saying "There's so much time in the day! We are so lucky!"

Possibility versus necessity

In NLP it is always useful to believe that choice is available. The use of modal operators creates a different energy when moving from impossibility to possibility.

E.g."I shouldn't do it this way", "I can't operate like this", "and I won't be able to do that shift".

"I intend to do it this way", "I can operate like this", I choose to do that shift"

Say each of the phrases to yourself and feel the difference inside. The second phrases are powerful and intentional whereby the first seem negative and improbable.

Don't have to	Replace with	Deserve to
Must not		Intend
Ought not		Permit
Shouldn't		Can
Couldn't		Choose to

So permit yourself to do what you can because you deserve it!

Creating Outcomes

It's important to know where you are heading. There are many great examples in the first half of the book to show you how people have achieved their outcomes.

The question to ask is "what do you want?" I cannot emphasis enough how important this question is! Many times I see clients and they can sit and tell me everything that they don't want and what is wrong with their life.

When asked the question "what is it that you want" I can see people stopping in their tracks, fumbling and mumbling their words.

STTTTrrreeetch

OK, come on. What is it that you want? What is it that you would like to achieve and when would you like to achieve it? Look at all areas of your life. Your career, your family, relationships, health and wellness, spirituality, personal growth. What do you want to do, be and have?

How do you see yourself in 6 months time, 1 year ahead, 3 years ahead? What are you doing? Who are you with?

Write these down and start to formulate some plans, just keep writing as you think of it and let the pen flow. We shall add some structure to it very shortly. Go on, create your future!

Outcomes/Goals/intentions

We have all been on those courses whereby we work out our outcomes and ensure that they are SMART. Well we need to ensure that they are exceptionally smart!

Using the keys to achievable outcomes questions we can ensure that we have 'covered off all angles' on the vision and have fleshed it out.

You want to set out a journey for yourself so you need to know where you are now and where you want to get to. By setting out your outcomes it really focuses the mind. Once we have ensured that these are the right outcomes for you then it sets your brain in motion in order for you to find the resources required in order to achieve.

The key questions

"What specifically do you want?"

Ok, I know that you have just worked on what you want. Let's look at specifics, really think about the specifics of what you are after. Be really specific e.g. say you said "I want more money" you could receive a penny extra and you would have more money. Probably not what you were intending. "I have £10,000 net extra money in my bank account" is a lot more specific.

"Where are you now?"

It's good to get a starting point. Ascertain where you are right now in order to find your starting position.

"What will you see, hear, feel, etc., when you have it?"

You want to get really sensory specific. What will you be seeing, what are you saying to yourself, are others saying anything to you? What sounds surround you? What are the key feelings you have when you have achieved this? Build a picture with all your senses to ensure your brain has a clear internal representation.

"How will you know when you have it?"

What evidence is required in order for you to know that you have achieved this? What HAS to have happened for you to know that you have definitely achieved your outcome?

"What will this outcome get for you or allow you to do?"

You need to ensure you want this wholeheartedly. In achieving this outcome, what will this give you? What will this outcome add to my life? Is it really right for me?

"Is it only for you?"

Is this only for me? Can I take total control of this outcome? Do I need anyone else in order to assist me to achieve it? Can I persuade anyone???

"Where, when, how, and with whom do you want it?"

In what contexts do you want this outcome? And, where and when don't you want it? Where, when, how and with whom do you not want it?

"What do you have now, and what do you need to get your outcome?"

What resources are required in order for you to achieve this? Do you know anyone else who has achieved this already and what can you learn from them? Have you ever done this or anything like it before? Would you be able to 'fake it til you make it'? i.e. act as if you have it?

"What will you gain or lose if you have it?"

Fundamentally, is this goal good for you and your life? What impact could this have on other areas of your life? Who else will it affect?

And here's some mind benders for you. I love these questions as they really make you look at your outcome from all different angles and give you a real contrast.

Deep breath, here we go.

"What will happen if you get it?"
"What won't happen if you get it?"
"What will happen if you don't get it?"
"What won't happen if you don't get it?"

All of these questions ensure your goal is SMARTER than SMART!
Really take your time over the questions and focus on your answers.

Make sure you follow these questions for every goal.

Your language is important in setting the achievement e.g. if your goal is to have a job with a certain salary avoid:
"I would like a job with a £50,000 salary by the end of this year".
Go for
"It is 30th November 2008 and I have an annual salary of £50,000".

I can see!

Visualisation is key. It is a powerful tool to know, in detail, a clear internal representation of your outcomes.

So, what's the picture you can see? How bright is it? Is it colour or black and white? Is it a movie? How big is it? What sounds are in it? Is it loud or soft? What feelings are associated with it? How intense are they?

Play about with it. When you brighten that picture, do you look forward to it more? What about if you added a little sparkle to it? Make this the most powerful and intentional picture that you can hold in your mind!

It's your achievement, make it the way *you* want it!

Denis Waitley and scientists worked with U.S Olympic athletes in the 1980s on a programme called Visual Motor Rehearsal. The research found that when an athlete competed in an event only in their mind, the same nervous reaction in the body occurred as when they did their event in real life.

Essentially, they surmised that the mind cannot tell the difference between an actual, real life event and a vividly imagined one.

Vision boards

A great way to work on your visualisation and outcomes is to create a vision board. Get a pin board and pull together lots of pictures and add them to it. Get some magazines, print off pictures from the internet, and write down your dreams/outcomes. Then, focus on this board every day. Take a picture of it with you, allow yourself to visualise this wherever you want. Make it a living, breathing item that is with you at all times. When you achieve something, take it of your board and add the next one! This is the law of attraction. Ask yourself what you want to attract into your life? Focus on this every day.

SSSSTTTRREEETTCCHH

Pull together a vision board with your outcomes and focus on this on a daily basis.

I'm like this person, I like this person

Have you ever noticed that you can get on with some people easier than others?

Have you ever noticed 2 people who are really close with one another, it's as if they are mirror images of each other in their actions; it's a dance.

Have you ever finished off your partners sentences or spoken what they were just about to say?
Well, that's rapport.

Rapport is a process of connectiveness. It's not necessarily liking someone; you can build rapport with someone who you have a difference of opinion with. You need to establish rapport; it's an essential ingredient for successful communication.

We instinctively start to build rapport with people especially when you are entering a new group, a new company. You start to find out about common experiences, where people come from, who they know.

Remember the last time you met someone new and then you found out they either knew someone else that you know or went to the same school. All of a sudden this person is like a long lost friend and you are getting on like a house on fire!!
Well, that's rapport!

When you are in rapport with someone you can be in disagreement with them and still relate with them, respectfully and with trust. It's about being able to see 'eye to eye' with people, a connection.

In NLP, we really break it down into a process and look at many elements.

In studies completed in the 1970s, one of which is research by Professor Mehrabian of the University of California (UCLA) looking at how live communication was received and responded to. The impact of your communication is dependent on 3 factors— how you look, how you say what you say and what you say.

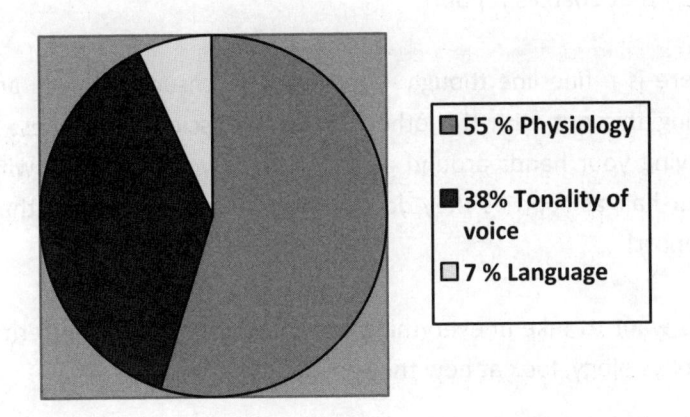

- 55 % Physiology
- 38% Tonality of voice
- 7 % Language

Your message is enhanced by you being in rapport with yourself, having all these elements work in harmony. 93% of our communication is unconscious, 93% of your message comes from *how* you say it.

Let's dance!

You can see the when people are in rapport with one another, they move easily and effortlessly in tune and in step with one another. You can also see when people are not in rapport, have you seen yourself in an argument or indeed witnessed an argument about service in a restaurant; the people are out of sync, completely out of time with one another.

Matching and mirroring is the key. It's listening with your *whole* body that enables rapport.

There is a fine line though – you want to ensure that you are doing this out with the other persons conscious awareness – waving your hands around as they talk to you or playing with your hair as soon as they do may lead to more of a fight than rapport!

You want to take in everything and match and mirror. In terms of physiology, look at how they are standing or sitting.

Visual people tend to have an erect posture, 'kinaesthetics' can be so laidback they are horizontal! What sort of handshake do they offer you – firm or the "wet fish"? Start to match and mirror their breathing, the location and pace of their breathing.

How close do they get to people? Some people have a wide dance space whereas others will be standing on your toes before they have realised there has been any 'violation' of personal space!

Look at their facial expressions, their smiles, their blinking.

What sort of tone of voice are they using? Is it a raspy voice or a clear succinct one? Are they **LOUD** or softly spoken? What words do they use? Do they speak in a rhythmic fashion as if there's a beat in their head that they are talking along to?

Listen to their language, are there any keywords, what predicates are they using (see the chapter on representational systems)?

By looking at all of these elements you will find that matching and mirroring will build a deep sense of rapport.

Building rapport and great relationships allows you to pace and lead the other person. In order to lead someone, you need to pace them first. Be patient, listen to them, acknowledge them and understand them. Leading is where you are attempting to get the person to change direction.

Listen and watch salespeople to see power of pacing and leading. A good sales person is one who listens, who acknowledges the need of the customer and what they really want.

I remember when I was due for an upgrade on my phone. After a telephone conversation with the telephone company about my upgrade I was sent the worst phone know to man! The man from the telephone company had built such good rapport with me- I was on the phone for forty five minutes-that it didn't matter what phone I had; infact I don't even think we discussed the phone until the last minute! Genius!

When I was buying my last car I trawled the car showrooms with my husband who duly pointed out all the different options to me. In one showroom I knew that I would never buy a car from there as the rapport building skills of the salesman were not that great! Granted, I could have built rapport with him although instantly I knew that this was never going to be my place of purchase.

Virtual rapport

With the virtual environment which we now live in with email, conference calling, Skype and the internet, it reduces face to face contact. We can build rapport over the telephone by the use of our voice.

Our voice is a fantastic tool which the majority of people do not use to the best of their ability. Match and mirror the other person on the other side of the call, their tone, quality, timbre, tempo of words. Listen out for any keywords and predicates that will enable you to 'hit their hot buttons'.

Think of the emails you are writing, what is the language you are using? Is it appropriately set out for the receiver? What predicates are necessary to build rapport with this person? In one company we worked in we did an exercise on representational systems. Those who had a high prevalence for Auditory digital would reply to emails succinctly and logically.

For example someone who is highly kinaesthetic receiving an email reply that says "noted" does not feel particularly comfortable!

SSSTTTTrretch

Start to notice people around you that are in rapport. What is it that enables that rapport? Are they matching and mirroring everything possible. Think about someone you are in rapport with, what elements have you been matching and mirroring?

Think about someone you are not in rapport with – what's the difference? What can you learn from the first person that you can use with the second?

Hear no evil, see no evil, feel no evil

You will have noticed that certain people respond to certain words. You will also have noticed that people move their eyes in certain ways when they are thinking.

In this chapter we are looking at **representational systems** and getting a sense for how people think internally.

Words are only 7% of our communication however what we will learn here is how to use words that are in certain representational systems.

Representational systems literally refer to representations of our experience – by choosing to pay more attention to information that comes through one sense rather than the other allows us to process our experience in different ways.

What are we representing?

These are your five senses through which we view the world. Visual – this is your sight system; Auditory – this is your hearing system; Kinaesthetic - your feeling system; Auditory Digital – your internal dialogue, your self talk; Gustatory – your sense of taste and Olfactory, your sense of smell.

Thinking back to the communication model, we take in information which is deleted, distorted and generalised by our filters and then we form an internal representation. This internal representation can be a picture with sound and feelings.

For the most part, the initial figures indicated roughly 40% of the people in the UK are visual, 40% are kinaesthetic and 20% are auditory and auditory digital exhibits characteristics of all these 3. We have carried out some research to look at the most recent figures. Our figures show 20% are auditory, 40% are visual and 40% are kinaesthetic. If you include Auditory digital then Ad is 35% and Auditory is 9% and Visual is 27% and Kinaesthetic is 29%.

Primary representational system

The primary comprises the predicates and physiology. How do they represent their internal world to the external world?

Lead representational system

This representational system relates to eye patterns (covered later in this chapter). How do they lead, how do they access their world internally.

Most of us have a preferred representational system – the highest order of responsiveness to the world with the system in which a person makes the most number of distinctions; where they are most comfortable.

STTREEttttccHHH

What's your preference?

For each of the following statements, please place a number next to every phrase.

Use the following system to indicate your preferences:

4 = Closest to describing you
3 = Next best description
2 = Next best
1 = Least descriptive of you

I make important decisions based on:
_____ gut level feelings
_____ which way sounds the best
_____ what looks best to me
_____ precise review and study of the issues

During an argument, I am most likely to be influenced by:
_____ the other person's tone of voice
_____ whether or not I can see the other person's point of view
_____ the logic of the other person's argument
_____ whether or not I am in touch with the other person's true feelings

I most easily communicate what is going on with me by:

_____ the way I dress and look
_____ the feelings I share
_____ the words I choose
_____ my tone of voice

It is easiest for me to:

_____ find the ideal volume and tuning on a stereo system
_____ select the most intellectually relevant point in an interesting subject
_____ select the most comfortable furniture
_____ select rich, attractive colour combinations

_____ I am very attuned to the sounds of my surroundings
_____ I am very adept at making sense of new facts and data
_____ I am very sensitive to the way articles of clothing feel on my body
_____ I have a strong response to colours and to the way a room looks

Results

Step One: Copy your answers from the previous page to here

1) _____ K   2) _____ A
   _____ A   _____ V
   _____ V   _____ Ad
   _____ A   _____ K

3) _____ V   4) _____ A
   _____ K   _____ Ad

_____ Ad
_____ A

_____ K
_____ V

5) _____ A
_____ Ad
_____ K
_____ V

Step Two: Add the numbers associated with each letter. There are 5 entries for each letter.

	V	A	K	AD
1				
2				
3				
4				
5				

Step Three: The comparison of the total scores in each column will give the relative preference for each of the 4 major Representational Systems.

There are key characteristics of the different systems.

Visual

People who are visual often stand or sit with their heads and/or bodies erect, with their eyes upwards .They will be breathing from the top of their lungs and often talk very fast. They often sit forward in their chair and tend to be organised, neat, well-groomed and orderly. Appearances are important to them and they are often thin and wiry. They memorise by seeing pictures and are less distracted by noise. They often have trouble remembering verbal instructions because their minds tend to wander.

A visual person will be concerned about how your program looks. They are not great fans of sales (far too messy!) and like their own space – don't get too close!

Key industries: PR, Marketing.

Kinaesthetic

People who are kinaesthetic will typically be breathing from the bottom of their lungs, so you'll see their stomach go in and out when they breathe. They often move and talk verrryyy slowly. They respond to physical rewards, and touching. They also stand closer to people than a visual person. They memorise by doing or walking through something. They will be interested in your program if it "feels right", or if you can give them something they can grasp.

Key industries: caring industries – therapy, nursing, massage

Auditory

People who are auditory will quite often move their eyes sideways. They breathe from the middle of their chest. They typically talk to themselves and can be easily distracted by noise. Some even move their lips when they talk to themselves.

They can repeat things back to you easily, and learn by listening, and usually like music and talking on the phone. They memorise by steps, procedures and sequences. TELL them how they are doing, they respond to a certain tone of voice or set of words. Auditory people will be interested in what you have to say about your program.
Key industries: Music industry.

Auditory Digital

People who operate within auditory digital exhibit characteristics of the other representational systems. They often need to repeat what you have said to them back to themselves therefore the response to your question may be quite slow; when they do this you will see their eyes move down and to the right. These people rehearse what they are going to say before they come into your office. They spend a lot of time talking to themselves inside their heads.
Key industries: IT, Accountancy, Lawyers.

What's' the word?

Some people like to visualise and see what you are talking about; these are visual people. Others like to get a feel for what you are saying and grasp the information; these people are kinaesthetic. Some people like to listen and hear what your proposal is; these people are auditory. Others prefer to make sense of the criteria; these people are Auditory digital

So, how can we use it?

For example, if you are calling me on the phone and I answer in a high pitch voice – it's probably more visual. If I answer the phone and I answer very low and slowly –either auditory or kinaesthetic. Listening to these you can begin to pick up on whether the person is Visual, Kinaesthetic or Auditory.

People who have quickly grouped words with lots of interruptions of um or ah probably were visual or auditory. People who were kinaesthetic or Auditory digital might have deliberate phrasing and or long or complicated sentences.

The processing pattern for a visual or auditory person might be quick with a minimum of detail and they might let you know unconsciously when they understand by changing the subject. Someone who is Kinaesthetic or auditory digital might want more detail and might not give you an indication of understanding unless you ask them.

In NLP our belief is that the descriptions that we use to describe what is going on in our head are not metaphorical descriptions – but they are actually real and accurate descriptions. If someone you are talking to says I don't see what you are saying. The truth is, they just don't see it.

That means they have not been able to make a picture in their head based on the information you have given them. If someone says to you what you are saying to me, doesn't sound right. It may be that your voice is not appropriate for them to decide that. If someone says I don't feel right you haven't given them enough information for them to have the right feeling inside of themselves. If someone says it just doesn't make sense then you haven't given them enough logical reasonable rational digital information for them to decide.

All this information enables us to build rapport with people and annotate our language to communicate more effectively. You see, we talk to people within our preferred representational system therefore it's no surprise to know that, sometimes, our information isn't received by others.
So, when you are talking to people, notice not just *what* they are saying but *how* they are saying it. Notice the predicates that they are using and change your language to incorporate more from the other person's representational system.
It works!

The next section talks about eye patterns which pulls together the representational systems and eye patterns. Working these both together is gold dust

The Eyes have it!

One of my biggest fascinations in NLP is in the recognition of eye patterns.

Have you noticed that people move their eyes when they are talking and when they are talking to you? Well, you will now!

This is going to take your people watching skills to a whole new level.

As with the representational systems, understanding eye patterns enables you to build rapport at a deeper level. They are also very important in strategies which we are going to talk about in this chapter.

Bandler and Grinder recognised that people moved their eyes in relation to what representational system they are accessing. It's as if there are certain filing cabinets stored in unique areas in our brain where we file relevant information.

So, by looking at other peoples eye accessing cues you can pretty much work out how they are going to answer your question; what sort of language they are going to use. You can then communicate with them in a way in which they respond positively e.g. if you know someone is accessing a picture in their head you can say, do you see what I mean? If they are accessing their feelings, you could say, does that feel right to you?

So, firstly let's look at the eyes.

Vc   Vr

Ac   Ar

K   Ad

Firstly what do the abbreviations mean?
Visual construct – someone is seeing new or different images.

Visual remembered – they are seeing images seen before.

Auditory construct – new sounds are being accessed.

Auditory recall – they are remembering sounds heard before.

Kinaesthetic – accessing of feelings, sense of touch, the domain of the emotions

Auditory Digital – is when the person is talking to themselves.

These eye patterns are as you look at a person. You can spend hours looking in the mirror endeavouring to work out your own eye patterns however it may begin to hurt rather a lot!

The majority of people will have this pattern of eye accessing cues; these people are invariably right handed. A small proportion who are generally left handed are reverse organised (the complete mirror image).

What you need to see...
Visual construct – the person looks up to *their* right (as you look at them to the left).

Visual remembered – the person looks up to *their* left (as you look at them to the right).

Auditory construct – the person looks to their left centre – across horizontally to the left.

Auditory remembered – the person looks to their right centre- across horizontally to the right.

Kinaesthetic – the person looks down to their bottom right.

Auditory digital – the person looks down to their bottom left.

SSSTTRREEttch

Now in order to practise this you want to be able to use your sensory acuity to calibrate. Some people's eye patterns are very pronounced whereas others you really need to be staring them out initially to pick them up!

It's all about practise and you want to be able to see them on an unconscious basis.

One of our students wrote to me with a fantastic story about winning a fluffy pink unicorn in a fairground by watching the eye patterns of the compere. The audience had to guess whether the next card was higher or lower than the last one, he got it every single time without fail by watching the eye patterns! See what you can achieve!

It's a good idea to grab some people (random or otherwise) and start to look at the eye patterns. Get really consciously competent first by asking questions that allows you to pick up on the movements. You want to be asking questions that get the other person to go far back in their filing cabinet. If the information is fairly close and recent for the other person they may just defocus therefore you want to ask questions initially that get the big movements.

Here's some example of questions:

Visual recall: What was the colour of your first bedroom? What was the colour of your first car? What does your first school uniform look like?

Visual construct: What would your bedroom look like if it were pink and purple tartan (assuming it wasn't pink and purple tartan in the first place! Yikes!) ? Picture a purple elephant.

Auditory recall: what were the first words you said today? What were the first words you heard today? What does Yoda from Star wars voice sound like?

Auditory construct: What would I sound like with Yodas voice? What would a dog sound like with an elephants trunk?

Kinaesthetic: What would it feel like to get into a bath full of baked beans? What is it like to get a hug from your favourite person (assuming the person likes hugs!)?

Auditory digital: What do you say to yourself when you make a mistake? Recite the eleven times table to yourself in your head

(Some people will access this visually, which is great retention- will cover this in learning strategies later).

So, go forth and practise being consciously competent.

Look at me when I'm talking to you!

Some people have a 'look to talk rule' which may, at first, seem as if they are hardly moving their eyes. You will begin to observe the minute details of change. Some cultures have a 'don't look to talk rule'. We have also found that people in the armed forces especially areas such as the SAS are very good at their poker faces! Look at everything about the person, there will be small analogically marked movements which denote the eye accessing cues.

As described earlier you can see how this will enable rapport. If you can see someone look up to their right, you can say "How does that look to you"; if they are looking down to their left, "Does that make sense to you now?"

Using the eye patterns in strategies

Strategies govern everything that we do. We have a strategy for all; our learning, getting out of bed in the morning, parenting, making decisions, buying, eating, and baking a cake – the lot!

We do not consciously think about how we do all of these things however they are all made up of a sequence of representational systems with certain submodalities.

They are *how* we do what we do. If these strategies are not working for us then we can change them.

If we know our buyers buying strategy we can sell to them in their strategy!

If there is someone that we really need to motivate we can motivate them by using the language from their motivation strategy!

Developing learning strategies are a key element in NLP in Education and I wish I knew a few of these skills when I was at school!

Types of strategies

Buying Strategies

Would it be useful to know your buyers buying strategy? I thought so! How they make the decisions unconsciously may be very different to how they are projecting it out loud. Love to shop? Some people can love shopping too much and can have huge credit card bills and clothes with labels still attached to them in your wardrobe, your buying strategy may not be working for you.

Decision making strategy

This is the way that you come up with a decision. Do you calmly and quickly reach decisions or do you go round and round in circles tiring out all those around you?

Motivation strategy

What has to happen in order for you to be motivated? Do you find it easy to get yourself to do something? If not, then perhaps a look at your motivation strategy will assist.

Learning strategy

This is *how* we learn. What sequences happen internally in order for you to learn and retain information? You may have different strategies for different subjects.

Love strategy

How do you become attracted to someone? How do you know they are attracted to you? How do you know when someone is in love with you? Anyone in a relationship would benefit from knowing your other halves strategy as well as your own.

Finding out the how

Now we are going to find out how to discover other people's strategies. You are going to require your rapport skills and your representational systems and eye patterns skills.

When you write down the steps in a strategy, the steps are generally abbreviated. Visual is written as V, Auditory is written as A, and Kinaesthetic as K, Auditory Digital (internal dialogue) is written as AD.

E.g., if a lady is telling you her buying strategy is,

"I went into the shop as it looked exciting, there was a sale on and I needed a new pair of boots for the winter, I tried on the first pair and they felt so comfortable and I bought them".

Her strategy can be written as;
V – Ad – K

STTTRREETTTCHH

These are the steps in eliciting strategies. As always, ensure you have rapport with the other person.

Can you recall a time when you were totally motivated/in love/learning well etc?
Can you recall a specific time?
As you go back to that time now what was the very first thing that caused you to feel motivated?

Was it something you saw? Was it the way someone looked at you? Was it something you heard? Was it the touch of someone or something? What was the very first thing that caused you to be totally motivated?
After you saw that, what was the very next thing? And so on until you have the strategy.

Spelling strategies

The key to learning is in visualisation. Pam and Julie (pages 24 and 33) both talk about using the strategies with their sons.
You want to hold up the item they need to learn in their visual recall. So, looking at them, they have it on their right hand side looking up. So they hold it in their left hand (if they are normally organised).

When they need to recall the word them they look back up to their left and they can see the word!

An expansion of this in the learning strategy is to link the three major modalities together. So, hold whatever it is up to your left so that you can see it, then say it out loud ('activating the auditory') and then look down to your right and get a feel for the answer.

I have used this every time I need to retain information and it works! If you write something that is inaccurate then your feeling is like a warning signal to you.

Planes, trains, chocolates and spiders!

Have you noticed that when you think of someone you like that you have a picture? What is the brightness of that picture? Are there any sounds there? What do you feel and what is the location of those feelings?

We talked about representational systems, our modalities, earlier. The **submodalities** are the fine tuning of the modalities. They give the extra detail to the modalities.

Examples of visual submodalities are brightness and focus; auditory submodalities are loudness and direction of sound; kinaesthetic submodalities are intensity and location of feeling. Submodalities are the finite detail of the pictures we hold in our minds. By changing the submodalities you change the meaning of the picture.

Think of the NLP Communication Model, if we change our internal representations, then we affect our physiology and state and behaviour.

Internal Representations
↕
State
↕
Physiology

Time/Space Matter/Energy
Language Memories
Decisions Meta Programs
Values & Beliefs
Attitudes

← **External Event**

↘ **Behaviour**

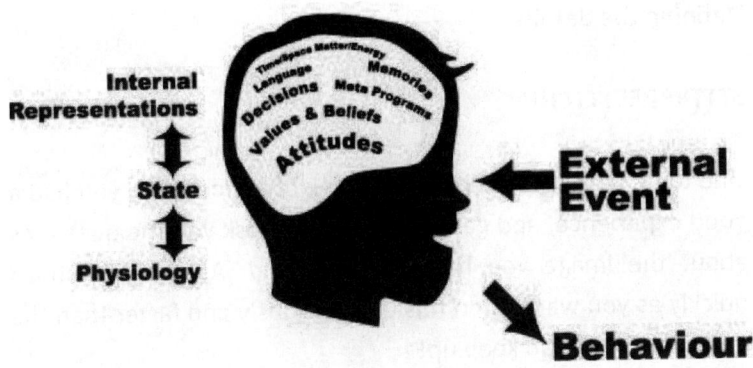

By changing a small detail of the images we hold in our minds, we can change limiting beliefs, our perception of certain foods, our behaviour and ultimately the results we have in our life.

STTRREEETTTCCHHHH

Close your eyes and remember a time when you were excited (or another pleasant experience). Yes you can! Remember a specific time when you were excited, float down into your body, look through your own eyes and ask yourself what do you see? As you think of the experience do you get a feeling? Do you hear any sounds?

Now take that picture and shrink it really really small and make it dark and push it away from you – far away out the house, office, car, room. Do you feel more excited?

No, I didn't think so! Well, bring it back and crank it up to maximum! Increase it so that you are VERY excited. Good, now you can come back! Hello? Whenever you are ready!

Defining the details

STTTRRREETTTCHH

One to do with a partner I think. Think of a time when you had a good experience, and get your partner to ask you the questions about the image you hold in your mind. Ask the questions quickly as you want to do this unconsciously and faster than the conscious mind can keep up!

Visual Submodalities	Questions to elicit
Black & White or colour	Is it black & white or colour?
Location	Is it near or far? Close to you? Point to it
Brightness	Is it bright or dim?
Size	What's the size of the picture? Is it small or big?
Associated or dissociated	Are you looking through your own eyes (associated) or do you see your body in the picture (dissociated)
Focus	Is the focus in sharp focus or is it fuzzy? Is the focus changing or steady?
Framed or panoramic	Does the picture have a frame round it or is it panoramic?
Movie or still	Is the picture still or is it a movie?

Also the sounds you hear have certain qualities. Again focus your mind and find out about the sounds in your head.

Auditory submodalities	Questions to elicit
What are they?	What are the sounds? Are they voices?
Location	Where are the sounds coming from? Point to where the sounds are coming from.
Direction	From what direction?
Internal or external	Are the sounds inside your head? Or external?
Loud or soft	Are the sounds loud or soft?

Moving onto the feelings we have in association with the picture, again asking the questions quickly.

Kinaesthetic submodalities	Questions to elicit them
What are they?	What are the feelings?
Location	Where are the feelings in your body? Point to them
Size	What size are they?
Shape	Do they have any shape?
Intensity	How intense are they?

Anytime you are working with submodalites, speed is of the essence, ensure you are discovering them quickly and make a list of them (the checklist we use is at the end of this chapter).

Changing your thoughts on food

A super fast and great technique you can do with submodalities is the like to dislike. There's been a few mentions of this technique (Osmaan and his fizzy sweets page 41,; Hilary and her Irn Bru page 36, and Kevin and his white wine, page 26). This is a two step process, starting with contrastive analysis and then mapping across.

Contrastive analysis is the comparison of two sets of submodalities e.g. with Hilary (page 36) she had the submodalities of Pepsi and then the submodalities of salt water. Salt water created a different feeling and would have a different set of submodalities. In contrastive analysis you are looking for the differences. The critical submodalities are the ones that when changed they affect the other submodalities. Location and association/dissociation (looking through your own eyes or seeing your body in the picture) can have a huge impact on the other attributes such as feeling and sounds. These are the drivers, the difference that makes the difference.

Mapping across is changing one set of submodalities into another. This is where you see the drivers working; you don't really know the key drivers until you do the process of mapping across.

STTTRRETTCHH

Grab your partner by the hand! And ensure you use the submodality checklist at the end of this chapter.

1. So, think of something you like but wish that you didn't. Got it? Good, so when you think about how much you like that, do you have a picture? Discover/elicit the submodalities using the checklist.
2. Now, can you think about something you dislike? When you think about how much you dislike it, do you have a picture? Discover/elicit the submodalities.
3. Clear the screen
4. Now, bring to mind the picture of the item that you like that wish to dislike. Then what you want to do is change the submodalities of the picture into the submodalities of that of which you like.

Changing limiting beliefs with submodalities

"I can't do that" or "I shall never earn enough money" and "I'm no good at languages" are all limiting beliefs. These are generalisations that can limit you and hold you back. Again, these thoughts will have a certain picture associated with them which means we can change that and then change the meaning.

STTTRRETTTCHHHHH

Again, a partner is required for maximum results and use your submodality checklist.
1. Think of a limiting belief that you currently hold that you would like to change. Discover the submodalities
2. Think of a belief for you that is no longer true. E.g. I am no longer sixteen. Or that Santa Claus no longer exists (only kidding!). Discover the submodalities.

3. Now change the submodalities of the limiting belief into the submodalities of that which you used to believe.

   Move it to the same location as the e.g. Santa Claus location, give it the same brightness etc etc

Now, let's create an empowering, desired belief.

4. Then think of a belief that is empowering/useful! E.g. it could be the opposite of number one
5. Now, think of a belief which for you is absolutely true e.g. the sun will rise tomorrow (even in Scotland!) or Santa Claus does exist.
6. Now change the empowering belief into the same submodalities as the one which is absolutely true. Move the useful belief into the same position as that rising sun.

SWWWIIISHHHHHH!!!

This submodality technique can make lasting change in minor negative states and behaviours. The swish pattern installs a new choice, it gives you an option. It teaches you a different way to respond instead of the unwanted behaviour.

If you want to stop biting your nails, or if you want to feel relaxed in presentations or talking to certain people (e.g. Colette and her wobblegob – page 74 . Wobblegob was a term phrased in a Manchester course. It refers to that feeling that you can get when you feel your voice going all wobbly, like you have swallowed a sheep, and your legs start to go all shaking Stevens! A beautiful terminology I find!).

You need to ensure you find the trigger for this one. E.g. how do you know it's time to bite your nails? Is it the feeling of the rough nail? That's the picture that you are going to change. It's the picture of the trigger.

SSTTRRETTTCHHH

Grab a partner and swish!

1. Identify the trigger that starts off the unwanted behaviour and know what that picture is. Break state.
2. How would you like to act/feel instead? This is your desired image, associate yourself into the picture (look through your own eyes) and play about with the picture until you are licking your lips! This is something you really want to do instead, its compelling! Then ensure you have the picture you want and step out of the picture so you see your body in the picture.
3. Then squash this desired picture and shrink it down and place it in your bottom left hand corner. Make sure you see your body in the picture.
4. Bring back the old picture and make sure you are looking through your own eyes and it is right in front of you.
5. Here comes the swish part! With a *swwiiishhhh* sound launch that dark image into the big picture so that it explodes, covering the old picture!

6. Break state
7. Then repeat step 5 and 6 as many times as required until you get the new picture only and the old trigger picture is gone.
8.

Planes, trains and spiders

Phobias are like anchors. If something has distressed us in some way and we have a reaction to them which is severe and irrational then it is a phobia. Apparently there are 530+ listed phobias documented in the world!

We have carried out research on the phobias we conduct within our courses and with clients. Spiders and planes crop up a lot closely flowed by snakes and rats.

The fast phobia model is a phenomenal technique. It is a submodality technique which scrambles the clients programming of the brain. It changes the representation of the item that we are phobic about.

What I have found in the research we have done is that a lot of phobias are genealogical e.g. you hear people say – "my mum was scared of spiders and my grandmother was too!" We teach our children phobias!

Many parents say they would like to get rid of their phobias as they can see their children reacting in the same way as they are.

With a phobia you have learned to do something again and again and again. When working with people it would be important to note that as this learning has taken place it means that the brain can learn to do something which is useful just as easily!

STTTTRRRETTTCCCCHH

Work with a partner on this as it is you may need to guide the person to be dissociated.
1. Ask the person to recall their phobia. Note any changes in physiology and emotions. Make sure they think about it quickly to ensure that they do not become associated with the emotion.
2. Break the state
3. Establish a resource anchor (see chapter on magic buttons and use a positive calming emotion and build a really strong resource anchor).
4. Ask the person to imagine they are in a projection booth and they are going to watch a movie.
5. Ask them to put the first event of the phobia onto the movie screen and they are going to run it forwards in

black and white all the way to the end, seeing their body in the picture. Run it all the way to end when they were safe.
6. Freeze frame
7. Then get them to associate into the memory (jump in from the projection booth) and run it backwards in colour all the way to the beginning as fast as they can.
8. Do this as many times as required until they feel calm and cannot access the negative emotion.
9. Test and future pace. How do they feel about the item they were phobic about? Are they OK? What will happen in the future when they come into contact with the trigger again?
10. You may want to do a swish pattern to give the person a new behaviour in the circumstance.

I did it!

"They couldn't stop me, I even completed the exercise Karen said she wouldn't. I was told I was like a squirrel climbing the tree and I walked on the log suspended 30 ft up between two trees. When I jumped off I shouted for them to take a picture and they left me suspended mid air while they searched for a camera. It felt fantastic.

Fear of heights, what fear of heights."
Pam had a fear of heights and, with a 10 minute (maximum) work on the fast phobia model. Gone.

Submodality checklist

Visual	1	2	3	4
Black & White or Colour?				
Near or Far?				
Bright or Dim?				
Location?				
Size of Picture?				
Associated/ Dissociated?				
Focused or Defocused?				
Focus (Changing/Steady)				
Framed or Panoramic?				
Movie or Still?				
Auditory: Location				
Direction				
Internal or External?				
Loud or Soft?				
Kinaesthetic:				
Location				
Size				
Shape				
Intensity				

Are there any sounds that are important, what are they??

Are there any feelings that are important, what are they??

Magic buttons

"I got out of bed the wrong side this morning"
"I just feel like everything is getting on top of me"
"I'm nervous about presenting to the board"

If you think back to the presuppositions of NLP then we are in charge of our state. It is our choice to be happy, sad, excited. It's impossible to be happy and angry at the same time so what would make you choose to be angry?

How would you like a magic button that, when pressed, gets you into the state that you require for the day?

An **anchor** is an unconscious trigger that can be applied to produce a positive state of mind and to change your behaviour. It allows us emotional freedom and the ability to access powerful positive states.

Anchors can allow you to function at your best in any situation, especially those where in the past; you may have felt negatively towards them. Again, in terms of presuppositions and beliefs for NLP is that we already have all the resources inside ourselves to be and get whatever we want. This allows us to grab hold of the resources when we want them.

Anchors work by creating an association, a link between an emotion and an external trigger.

Behavioural psychologists say that our life is a series of conditioned reflexes to anchors. Ivan Pavlov, the famous Russian psychologist experimented with this with the dogs and the steak. He would ring a tuning fork at the same time as handing the dogs a steak. Then, afterwards, he would ring the tuning fork and the dogs would start to salivate. The dogs were now conditioned and they linked the stimulus of the tuning fork to being fed. Therefore, when they heard the sound, their internal representations were that of being fed, which, in turn, changed their state and then their physiology.

Sensory anchors.

Think of it – what do you do when the phone rings? What do you do when you see a red light? I hope you stop!
Music is a great auditory anchor. When we hear certain music it can "take us back" to when we last heard it. If we were in an intense, associated state when you heard the music, hearing it again can trigger that state off again. There's a certain type of music that can transfer me back to my wedding; I can see

everything around me, feel the feelings and hear the words. It's great!

Children's TV programmes create strong visual and auditory anchors. I have watched my niece stop in her tracks when she hears the theme tune to 'Balamory' or 'Bob the Builder'.

Olfactory anchors are also powerful. Think of what people tell us to do when we are selling her house – bake fresh bread, put on a warm pot of coffee and allow the aromas to radiate through your home. The smells of fresh bread in a supermarket acts like a pied piper and the lure of Starbucks is strong when you begin to smell the freshness of the coffee.

Visual anchors are all around us. Advertising is a powerful tool in creating anchors. Think of the Apple logo, coca Cola sign, the upside down wave – Nike! A smile, a frown, a hand gesture are all visual anchors.

Kinaesthetic anchors could be the touch of someone, a hand on the back, a hug or the feel of fresh sheets and your "own bed" after being away from home. Or wearing your favourite dress or "lucky pants"!

These triggers are all around us and they have an effect on our state. We can create our own triggers to be in charge of our state. There are several processes in anchoring, we are going to talk about resource anchors and collapse anchors within this chapter. Both are powerful techniques and allow us to be completely in charge of our state.

Creating magic buttons

Chuckle knuckles!

The phrase chuckle knuckles has been used a few times in the first part of this book (pages 26, 37, 51, 90)! In many of our courses students anchor the state of anchor and usually we are using the knuckles as part of the anchoring process. I think the term came from a course last year in Manchester and has stuck with me throughout all of our courses so there are now chuckle knuckles up and down the country keeping people happy in their work!

People go into states in different ways. For some people, mention the word laughter and they are rolling around the floor holding their sides. For others, they need to a bit of time to "get into" the state, they need to take time to think about what they saw, what they heard, how they felt.

As we all take times to go into states, we also all stay in the state for different periods of time. When anchoring we really need to use our sensory acuity and focus on the person to witness the change in their breathing, physiology, skin tonus etc.

Applying an anchor

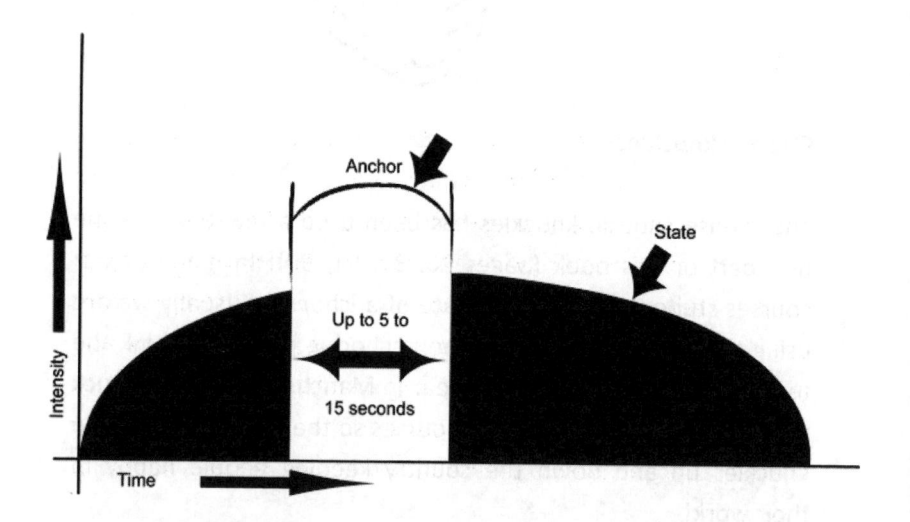

Intensity ↑
Time →

Anchor
State
Up to 5 to 15 seconds

We want to be applying the anchor before the peak. What kind of anchor? If you are working with someone in the application of their anchor then decide what kind of anchor you would like to use – visual, auditory, kinaesthetic.

Working one on one, you can touch the person on the knuckle when you see them just before the peak of the state. You want the anchor to be unique and the knuckle is not normally touched that often (check with the person if use their hands a lot e.g. martial arts).

You can still use the anchor, ensure that they are appropriate! Having a chuckle knuckle may not be right for the middle of a fight contest!

Also, normarily we want to hold the anchor for up to 5 to 15 seconds. If we apply an anchor just at the peak then we have lost the strongest part of the state.

Resource anchor

A resource anchor is a great tool to enable you to bring positive resources into a situation. I have several different resource anchors set up which is a good idea. You could have a resource anchor for positive "lively" states and another one for "relaxed, chilled". A resource anchor can have several different states "stacked" in one place. If you were to add "excitement and motivation" and then add in "calm" you may find it difficult to access one of or more of the states as the calmness may have been so powerful and 'washed away' the excitement and motivation.

Think of some positive states now that you would like to be able to access. E.g. motivated, excited, enthusiastic, confident, powerful, laughter, relaxed, calm, blissful....

STTTTTTrrreeetch

Here we go! This is how to set up a resource anchor.

If you are working with someone else then it is important that you have rapport with that person. When you have rapport, you can get into the state too, which will allow the other person to access the state easily.

Watch your client and ensure you apply the anchor before the peak of the state.

So,
1 Firstly, ensure you are in rapport with your client and access the state yourself.
2 elicit the state with your client, get them to recall a time when they were e.g. excited, a specific time, float into their body, looking through their own eyes and see what they saw, hear what they heard and feel what they felt.
There are differing intensities to states; the most powerful being a naturally occurring state – it's happening *now* and you anchor right at that moment. Secondly, is as here, the recalling of a state – what is it that you saw, heard or felt? And thirdly, for some people they need to have time to construct the state. How would they stand or sit when they felt excited? What would they be seeing? Would they be saying anything to themselves?
Watch your client and anchor the state just before the peak and hold.
3 if you want to stack the states then continue to add more and more states (ensure the states are 'aligned" in that they are similar in nature).
4 Change state – get the person to focus their attention on something else in order to break their state.
5 and then press the knuckle again to get the person back into the state. This is called firing the anchor – setting it off. With this kind of kinaesthetic anchor you would touch the anchor for a

few seconds to trigger off the feelings. What happens? If you have anchored correctly, you will see the other person get into the state through the change in their physiology etc. If you have anchored yourself you will feel the change internally. How do you feel? Is it different? Is it strong, compelling enough? If not, go back and anchor some more!
5 Future pace the use of the anchor. Think of a time when in the past it felt unresourceful or negative. In imagining firing of the anchor, how different does it feel?
A resource anchor is useful within sports. In working with golfers, we set up anchors on their clubs in order for them to be in charge of their state whilst taking the shot.

Anchoring self

People always ask if it is possible to anchor yourself. I have a resource anchor on my ear which I use when I am in a positive intense state. So, any time I am in a powerful, intense state I squeeze my ear thus anchoring the good state. In essence my ear is huge as I have a massive amount of positive anchors stacked one on top of another!

Anchors away!

Collapse anchors can be use to get rid of negative states and sets up new choices.
By anchoring two sets of states and then firing them both off at the same time, the weaker one collapses into the stronger one.
Imagine you got irritated when in a queue, frustrated when you got to a certain point in your training.

Sttrrreeetttcccchhh

This will create a feeling of neutral emotion. What you want to do is stack positive states in one place (just like you did with the resource anchor) and then anchor the negative state once.

1. Again, ensure you are in rapport with your client.
2. Stack the positive states in one place. It may be a good idea to use states that are similar together. E.g. imagine you wanted to collapse the anchor of 'feeling annoyed when you are stuck in a traffic jam' you could use positive states such as calm, relaxed, understanding etc.
3. Anchor the negative state once in a different place. If you are using the knuckles again, you could use the knuckle next to your positive one.
4. Change state
5. Then you are going to fire off both the anchors at the same time. This really is the fun part. Working with your partner, notice the changes. You will witness some asymmetry as the integration takes place – e.g. perhaps the person's eyes will be twitching, their feet tapping, their breathing changing. You want to keep applying the anchors (i.e. ensure you are holding both, or if doing a visual anchor – showing them both). When you see that the integration has occurred, release the negative anchor.
6. Hold the positive for a further 5 seconds.

7. Break state.

8. Test by asking how they are going to react instead.

Collapse anchors are fantastic for releasing minor negative emotions.

Circulating excellence

A really smart form of anchoring is with the circle of excellence. It's also a good one to do with a group of people. I know many people who use it to summon up the confidence when taking part in a presentation or indeed when they want to play their best in their sport. Again it's a stacked anchor that you can stack as many times as you would like.

SSTTRRRREEETTTCHH

Think of the situation where you are going to perform and imagine you have a magic circle about 1.5 metres in diameter in front of you. This is also a good exercise to do with a partner.

So, think of a positive state and remember a time when you were totally x'd (use the person's words) and see what you saw, hear what you heard and feel what you felt.
Step into the circle and relive the experience.
Now, when feelings start to decrease, step out of the circle.
Again, think of a positive state and remember a time when you were totally x'd and see what you saw, hear what you heard and feel what you felt.
You can repeat this as many times as you like.

Then imagine that circle decreasing in size whilst retaining its power. Decrease it to the size of a ring which you can slip onto your finger.

You now have the ring of power which you can take with you wherever you go! Whenever you need it, you can flick your ring onto the floor, expand it and then step into it, reliving and feeling all those positive states!

Anchors in business

As we use anchors to be in charge of our state and allow ourselves to access resources then we can use these in business. Spatial anchors are a way of using areas/the stage/ in a positive way and are persuasive in presentations.

Picture this, you are at your annual sales conference and the new sales director comes up on stage and starts to talk about the dismal performance of the past year. He stands in one spot whilst talking about the lack of profit and need for extra resource. Then he starts to talk about how this year is going to be different and the company is 'turning the corner', remaining rooted to the same spot.

He has already anchored all the bad news there and now he has added in the good news, this can dilute his message and intent. By moving to a different spot to talk about this years' new challenges and expected turnaround in performance he breaks your attention away from the bad news. Simple, yet effective.

Another key spatial anchor during presentations is the location of the projector screen. Invariably the screen is centre stage and, often there is a lectern off to the side for the speaker to plant themselves.

Ideally, you want to have the screen off to the left (as you look at the stage) as it is then firmly planted in the Visual recall section of the audience. Even more ideal is to have two screens that are on either side of the "stage".

Come Fly with me

past....................present....................future?

Do you find you are rushing and never have enough time?

Do you often find yourself late for meetings or do you get frustrated if someone is 2 minutes late for an appointment?

Are you stuck in the past, always comparing to 'what was once' or are you firmly focused on the future and all it brings?

Time can change meanings of memories, people have different thoughts and notions about time and how we represent it. We are all made up of a stack of memories, good or bad.

When you woke up this morning did you know what age you were? Were you able to know straight away the age you are now? By that very token, our memories must be organised in some sense in relation to time, this is what we call our timeline. More about that later.

Our unconscious mind, as we know, is a powerful tool and the domain of our emotions. If we have a lot of negativity in that domain then it can affect what happens to us in the present and the future.

I used to be a runner and my coach would put a huge piece of elastic around my waist and he would hold onto the back of it as part of my resistance training. I would still be able to move forward however at a much slower pace and oftentimes, not in the straightest of lines. Sometimes my coach would get more people to add onto the band and I would move slower and slower and slower.

Negative emotions and limiting decisions are like the elastic band. They can hold us back from achieving all that we can achieve. They can cause us to hold back or miss opportunities.

The Gestalt

All your memories are arranged in a gestalt. The gestalt is a collection of memories around a certain subject. We have gestalts for all of our emotions. So associated memories start a gestalt, you will have a gestalt for all of your emotions e.g. anger, happiness, sadness, joy. You have one event which triggers an emotional response (this is the root cause; the first event) and then another which is similar with similar emotion then the two become linked. This continues to happen until a chain is formed. I like to think of it as a string of pearls as per William James (1890).

When doing work with timelines, you go back and release emotions on the first event, it's as if you are removing the first pearl and the rest can just fall off the string.

Your organisation of time

Here we are going to find out *how* you store time.

STTRREEETTTCHH

This is a form of active imagination – we don't have timelines sticking out of our heads and hitting people as we walk past them. However if I were to ask you where your past is I have an idea that you might point to your right or left or up to down or in some direction in relation to your body and it's not your conscious concept that I am interested in, it's your unconscious. So, if you were to point to your past to what direction would you point? And your future, to what direction what you point if I were to ask you where your future was??

Or think about an event in the past, do you notice where it comes from? Think of an event that is going to happen in the future, do you notice that it has a different location?
Great, you have just found your timeline.

Everyone has a different configuration of time and the different configurations can be linked to certain personality traits.

Through time:

Some people's timeline is right out in front of them and it's as if they can see "through time". You may be very aware of the value of time, you probably have a diary or are intimately related with your Microsoft outlook calendar! You can be great at planning activities and very well organised. 'Through timers' can be quite dissociated and can keep emotions separate from events.
A classic through time phrase is time is on my side.

In time

In timers follow more of the Caribbean or Arabic notion of time e.g. manyana! (Infact the publishers know the author of this book is very much an intimer!).

Their timeline goes through them; they are caught up in time. This can also be what intimers may say "I was just caught up in time" or "you are going to look back on this and laugh!" They can often be late, they do not have the through time value of time philosophy. They are very associated and feel their emotions very strongly; they like to keep their options open and can often suffer buyer's remorse. Intimers are good multi taskers and can be very creative. They very much live in the moment, in the now.

SSSTTTRRRREETTTCHH

First let's have a test flight! Now, this is not a conscious process, your conscious mind has full permission to take a wee holiday for now as you relax. It may be a good idea to get someone to work with you here so that you can float above your timeline and they can direct you.
So, goggles on, silk scarves at the ready, chocs away!
Get yourself to a place where you won't get disturbed and relax. Get comfortable and close your eyes. Now, what I would like you to do is imagine yourself floating up above your timeline, now make sure you are looking through your own eyes and you are looking down on yourself in the now.

(It's important to note that Time Line Therapy™ is not purely a visual process, it can be kinaesthetically and auditorally. Obviously it is a construct, a form of active imagination, you're not really floating, and you are still seated!).

Now, floating above your timeline I want you to float back into the past and back to an event in the past, one that made you smile. Notice the emotions present, now float way above your timeline so your timeline is just like a little dot, *really really high!* Now, let's go and float above another time in the past, a time that made you laugh or you were excited about. Again, notice the emotions that are present and then just float above your timeline at a point at which you are comfortable.

Now, float out into your future, to an insignificant time and then come back to now.

Changing the timeline

To participate in the quickest time management course ever you can switch your timeline. As our timelines give us certain traits we can change these traits by changing our timelines. This can confuse people and can affect them very strongly.

Say, for example, you were an intimer with a job that required you to be organised and at lots of meetings, you could switch your timeline for work time and then switch it back for personal time. Someone who was very organised through timer could switch their timeline to a classic intime where they could become more relaxed and associated with the now.

Normally during our course we shall get people to change their timeline just before a lunch break. It is hilarious to watch! All the 'previous intimers' keep checking their watches and double checking when we are meant to be back from lunch! The 'previous through timers' are sitting around looking very relaxed and when asked what time lunch finished their reply is "whenever"!

SSTTTRREEETTCHH

Again, get ready to float! Take whatever provisions necessary and chocs away!

Floating above your timeline take a mental snapshot, a picture of how it is now. Then change the orientation of your timeline. If it's intime currently, then take it and stretch it out horizontally in front of you from left to right or right to left. If it's through time currently then take the timeline and put it through you from front to back so that you need to turn your head to see the timeline behind you. Then, come back to now.

It's as easy as that.

Time Line Therapy™ techniques

Dr Tad James has invented these successful techniques of Time Line Therapy™ that allow people to release negative emotions and limiting beliefs. It also allows us to programme our future. We can use our timelines to release negative emotions and limiting decisions. Think of something that has happened in your past that may have given you some negativity – as you look back on it now you feel OK about it as you have got the learning's in relation to this so this is a natural process that we already do.

Our unconscious mind ensures that we are protected and represses any memories with negative emotions. It can take a lot of energy for us to ensure this repression continues. Why repress? Because sometimes it's too big for us to deal with and then sometimes we just don't have time.

The process doesn't mean that people have to go back and "relive" any event or trauma in their past; it ensures that they receive the learning's and, in turn, release the negative emotions.

We have, in our heads, many filters. Our memories are one of those filters. The filters determine our experience. Think about it, if your memories have limiting decisions and negative emotions attached to them then this will affect our current experiences.

What Karen realised (page 44), by using the process of Time Line Therapy™ that she there was an unconscious decision that she made when young to get her out of an emotional time. She then created a habit and acted it out time and time again. Albeit we laughed a lot when she found out about it, it's another example of how our mind works!

Tracey also talked about the use of Time Line Therapy™ (page 60) and the effect it has had on her. She feels 'free of the past' and contented.

The major emotions

With Time line Therapy™, the emotions that we release are major negative emotions e.g. Anger, Sadness, Fear, Hurt, Guilt. These emotions can have a strong mental effect on our lives as well as a strong physical consequence. Releasing these emotions is powerful and can release a lot of energy from the body.

Have you ever worked with emotional vampires? Well, think of the effect that that has on your body, you feel tired, lethargic even stressed. Sometimes it's as if the very life has been sucked out of you. Well, if that's an external factor affecting you in such a way, think of what is happening to you when you keep all your negative emotions bottled up!

IMPORTANT: I think that anyone who is going to be working with Time Line Therapy™ should work with a qualified Time Line Therapy™ Practitioner or Master Practitioner especially if there's some really heavy duty stuff that needs to be released.

Phobias

We can use Time Line Therapy™ before the fast phobia model. Some people find that their phobia goes after working on fear with Time Line Therapy™; others find that it is still there. This means that they have a separate gestalt for their phobia. We can use Time Line Therapy™ to get back to the first event.

In the future

We can also use our timelines to create our future. So, any outcomes that I have worked on I ensure I build a strong internal representation of these and then insert them into my timeline. This is a really powerful process and really sets your RAS in motion!

The value in knowing your values

Have you ever wondered why you are not achieving the goals you have set for yourself?

Been really conscious about what you want to achieve and when however it just doesn't seem to happen?

In recruitment, have you ever hired someone and you know you have ticked all the boxes and then find that they have left the job you have recruited them for quickly?

In sales would it be important for you to know your buyers values so that you can feedback any proposal or project within what is important to *them*?

As you will remember from the introduction our values are one of the filters that do the process of deleting, distorting and generalising.

Values are what are important to us. It's not necessarily what we like but what's important to us; even if we hate something we may still do it.

Values have 2 purposes - creating who we are and what we do and they determine how we spend our time (you won't do something that is not important to you) and they determine our evaluations – whether what we did was right or wrong/good or bad.

They determine how we feel about self or others. They are more conscious then meta-programs and more unconscious than beliefs. Values create our motivation; what do we need to do with our time.

Where do they come from?

According to Morris Massey (Book – People Puzzle, 1970) values are formed during 3 major periods in our life. Age 0-7 year is the imprint period. You hear parents say "he's like a sponge" this is because at this age children are mainly little unconscious minds running around!

A lot of our values and perceptions are formed during this period. Our main influencers are our parents, and then we enter the modelling period (age 7-14 years) where we have additional influences as we go to school. In the modelling period you are looking for heroes. Who was your hero at that age? Whose poster did you have on your bedroom wall, who did you idolise? Between the ages of 7-14, we look at this as our modelling period.

Ages 14 – 21 is named as our socialisation period. Our circle of influence is ever increasing; we are meeting new people (who all have different values and priorities) and exploring new values options. A lot of our relationship values are formed at this age too and we can be more critical in our judgement of values as we determine our place in society.

William James added our business persona between the ages of 21 and 35 whereby we are starting to formulate work and career values.

We are influenced by many factors throughout our life – from family to school to our relationships with the media. Values come from a number of different arenas; you will either match them or mismatch them (Anyone with children in their teens may be experiencing strong mismatching at this point!).

In your family (even unconscious family values e.g. how your father was with your mother in terms of difference etc) and friends. Church/religion forms an important value set with some as does school where we are interacting with children from different backgrounds, how did the teacher react with you at school? Geography and economic times influence our values – clear differences in value sets are discovered when you move country or even town!

And more than ever media is responsible for a formation of values which like the headlines, changes on a daily basis!

Carrot or stick?

We can have toward values or away from values.

Let's look at an example of this;

If we are moving towards prosperity; that is where our focus is – prosperity. If however we are moving away from poverty then our motivation is getting away from poverty. Therefore when we get far enough away from poverty, we lose our motivation. People who have away from values have inconsistent results because as soon as they lose their motivation, they create something (consciously or unconsciously) that gets them back nearer poverty to get their drive and motivation back.

A great example of this is a famous entrepreneur. His first wife was interviewed by People magazine saying "We review everything we have on a daily basis as we know at any point it can be taken away from us". Now that's focusing on what you don't want, not what you want. Now he has had many peaks and troughs in his career (admittedly the troughs are slightly higher in value than my peaks!!!) however it shows inconsistency.

Language is key here. Do you work because you strive to be prosperous and successful or do you *not* want to be poor? This 2 stage process is such that our brain looks at being poor first. We need to ensure we use clean, positive language. Listen to what people say;

"I *don't* want to be fat"
"I *can't* be alone"
"I *should* study for my exams"
"I *don't* want to poor"
"I want to be *better* at my health and be *more* committed to it"

You want to be on alert for any negations (not, don't, wont) and comparisons (better, more, easier) and modal operators of necessity (should's and shouldn'ts). These are all indicators of possible away from motivators.

"I desire to be toned and slim"
"I can be alone. I see myself in a loving relationship"
"I aim to be successful and prosperous"
"I am focused on being committed to my health"

are indicators of toward motivations. Notice the difference, say them to yourself, they *feel* different inside.

STTRrrEEETCH!

So, what's important to you? Take some time and work out what is important to you. Do this within context e.g. what's important to you about your career? Or your relationship etc your life values are what you deem to be most important about your entire life. Your relationship values determine what kind of relationship you look for, your career values determine what kind of job you would enjoy.

Then find out your motivation values which may add more of your unconscious values into the mix e.g. can you remember a time in your e.g. career that you were motivated? What was it about that specific time that caused you to be motivated? Is that of value to you? Ask this as many times as you can until you run out of new words.

Doing this will give you a real insight into why things are happening in your life the way in which they are.

I had a client who was working on their values and focusing on their whole life values. One of her worries was that she wanted a boyfriend however wasn't sure why she didn't have one. We listed her values, looked at her motivation and threshold values and then sat back and looked at the list. What was apparent to me, unfortunately not to her, was that a boyfriend wasn't on the list. That *could* be a fundamental factor! She hadn't been focusing on that at all, she deemed it as unimportant. Even having that self awareness allowed her to get her act together and find a suitable man!

Another client was unsure about what he wanted from life and whether to stay at university or focus on a career. We focussed on his career values which was something that he had never done. He surprised himself by adding in certain elements and left. We had a follow up session a few weeks later where he arrived in a suit full of the joys of spring.

He had started a new job and was really happy with it, infact it was really challenging, he was able to help people and gain new experiences in it etc etc. I then handed him a printed copy of his values and he stopped in his tracks.

Every single item that he had just described was there in black and white. He laughed and said "Wow, I didn't do that consciously. I've just found a job that I described 2 weeks ago with my values!"

Again, by promoting that self awareness and taking time out to really think about what he wanted allowed him the break he needed. His brain was then 'activated' to go out and find something that met the necessary requirements. Magic!

What are you googling?

Think of it like a search engine. What are you focusing on? Are you focusing on what you want or what you don't want? If you are focussing on what you don't want your mind will go out and find it for you. The search engine has been activated and will search through all the pages until it find a perfect match ie exactly what you don't want!
Rearrange the search engine focus to what you want.

Applications

From the stories and achievements from all of the students you can see that the techniques covered in NLP can be use in various arenas and that's the beauty of it! Its a toolkit for many areas of our life and can create change in our personal and business life.

Business

Communication is paramount in every business and it pays to do it well.

Whether you are communicating with clients or colleagues, NLP defines *how* we communicate. We often get "bogged down" in the content – the "what". If we can listen to how people are talking to us we can make a difference. Using rapport we can work with the other persons' model of the world.
In sales, rapport is essential. Understanding your client's decision making strategy is of great value. Strategies allow us to understand your buyer on a deeper level, their convincer - how they need to be convinced and how to convince them.

When we were buying our car, I was sitting people watching (being nosy) and listening to sales people talking with potentially buyers. It was at the point when our sales guy was working out the numbers and I had tuned out and I heard a conversation between a buyer and a salesman.

"Well, the numbers look alright to me, I would like to have a look at the car again and see the space available.
"Certainly Sir, let's have a walk over and get a feel for the car"
"Actually, I'll come back later"
It took everything I have not to jump out of my seat and grab the buyer! The mismatching of predicates had turned him off.

Values are key within businesses. Especially if the person's values are misaligned with the company, this can create apathy, stress, lack of motivation etc.

In recruitment, it's of paramount importance to look at the values of the company and personnel fit. Also in recruitment, understanding of motivation strategies and metaprograms will assist in succession planning, enhance communication and enable management.

Educating Education

The use of key components can assist children. Personally I think sharing these techniques with children is a gift, I certainly wish I knew this when I was younger. Learning strategies and visualisation are key in education, along with the learning state.

We know a few teachers who use learning strategies with their pupils in assisting them with dyslexia.
"We have one girl in our year who is dyslexic in every other class except ours!"

The learning state and learning strategies can lead to a grade point average increase! Simple techniques with huge impact!

Even the teaching of the mindset and how we communicate are of paramount importance when younger.

Sport

Nowadays athletes are considering mental strength alongside the physical. More and more you hear about top sports peoples employing sports psychologists and "Mental gurus".

Anchoring is used within sport – think of Tiger Woods and his red t-shirt on the last day of a competition. Sir Clive Woodward was reported to have used certain techniques within the England Rugby team, think of Johnny Wilkinson and his "pose" before a conversion. All anchors.

We have worked with several golfers and set anchors on their golf clubs, therefore every time they use those certain clubs they are in the relevant state. Visualisation is key.

Therapy

All of the techniques discussed in this book we use with personal clients. People come to see us for many different challenges.
Weight loss – you could use work on finding the root cause with the meta model and using submodalities like to dislike.

Smoking cessation – usually a lot of emotional work is required for smoking however I know people who have successfully stopped smoking after a like to dislike or a swish. This has worked for "Social smokers" and to great effect.

Outcomes – some people do not actually know what they want out of life and are unsure of their direction. Working on the key mindsets and values and the keys to an achievable outcome enables them to unlock their thoughts.

Phobias – we work with phobias a lot, using the fast phobia model – effective and powerful.

Any number of challenges can be released using NLP as NLP allows us to create different internal representations and results.

So, whatever your interest in NLP you will find a technique, or a mindset to assist you. Enjoy the journey!

Index

A

Applications 224
Anchors 26, 51,110,194-226
~Chaining 31, 51,105
~Collapse 37,47,56
~Resource 59,199

B

Business 26,41,56,71,75,86, 88,108,115,138,204,224

C

Cause & Effect 24,27,39,41, 49,56,61,68,129

E

Education 24,27,49,84,225
Eye Patterns 165,172-177

H

Hypnotherapy 113

L

Language 33,61,94,133-150
~Meta Model 61,141-145
~Metaphors 27,110,136-140
~Milton Model 117,145-147

L

Law of Attraction 26,64,66, 76,105,113,122
Logical Levels of Therapy 90

M

Mind Set 24,26,27,39,41,49, 55,56,57,59,61,68,86,94,113,115,122

O

Outcomes 30,39,41,49,57, 64,66,74,82,88,90,105,122, 123,151-157

P

Parts Integration 41,79,88
Phobias
~Fast Phobia Model 41, 44, 47,51,53,68,74,82,90,113,119,190-192
Presuppositions 49,61,68,20-22

R

Rapport 69,115,158-163

RAS 132
Representational Systems 33,164-181

S

Sport 30,108,225
Strategies
~Buying 178,180
~Decision 179
~Learning 24,33,179,181
~Love 179
Sub modalities
~SWISH 37,47,74,82,120, 188-190
~Like to Dislike 26,36,38, 41,74,77,186-187
~Belief Change 37,47,79, 187-188

T

Therapy 27,33,47,51,71,79, 82,84,86,108
Time Line Therapy 27,30, 37,39,44,61,82,90,99,105, 110,118,119,123,206-215
~Gestalt 207
~Negative Emotions 39,214-215

V

Values 39,61,86,127,216-223
Visualisation 84,88,108,115,156-157

Great books & resources for you

Presenting Magically
Tad James & David Shepard

Purple Cow
Seth Godin

Need to know NLP
Collins

Seeing Spells Achieving
Olive Hickmott & Andrew Bendefy

NLP for Dummies
Romilla Ready & Kate Burton

Spiral Dynamics
Beck Cowan

The Story Factor
Annette Simmons

Tales for Trainers
Margaret Parkin

Sporting Excellence
Ted Garratt

The Secret
Rhonda Byrne
(audio, book and DVD)

Using your brain for a change
Richard Bandler

Structure of magic Vol I & II
Bandler & Grinder

Time Line Therapy & the basis of personality
Tad James

Hypnosis: A comprehensive guide
Tad James

NLP Coaching.com
Dr Tad & Adriana James

Time Line Therapy™ association
www.tltinfo.com

Thanks to

Voltage
www.powerfulstuff.co.uk
for the front cover design
Steve (thanks for bashing up some pink and throwing in some barcodes) and Scott – thanks!

Barry Thomson
For the illustrations – you are a lifesaver! Thanks.